First published in Great Britain in 2020 by:
Carnelian Heart Publishing Ltd
Suite A
82 James Carter Road
Mildenhall
Suffolk
IP28 7DE
UK

©Samantha Rumbidzai Vazhure

www.samantharumbidzai.co.uk

Editor: Daniel Mutendi

Cover image: Galushko Sergey
Image on page 3: Lindwa
Images on page 29, 55, 61 by: Irina Levitskaya

A CIP catalogue record for this book is available from the British Library.

PAPERBACK ISBN 978-1-8380480-2-0

All rights reserved. No part of this publication may be reproduced, stored in a retrieval system or transmitted in any form or by any means, electronic, mechanical, photocopying, recording or otherwise without prior written permission from the publisher.

Cover design by Daniel Mutendi & Samantha Rumbidzai Vazhure. Typeset by Carnelian Heart Publishing. Layouts and formatting by DanTs Media

Carnelian Heart Publishing

UPROOTED

Samantha Rumbidzai Vazhure

Table of Contents

10. *Introduction*
12. *Editor's note*
15. *Acknowledgements*

18. Your Highness VaChifedza
20. Uprooted
22. When will you return?
25. Voice box
26. My Lord
28. Misfortune
30. Adversity
32. Damn it!
34. Mother's tongue
36. Apparitions
37. MaTanzaniya
38. Prisoner of stuff
39. Ego
40. Evil spirit
41. Take this needle
42. Dare me!
43. Morningstar
44. Bones
45. Messengers
46. Jackal
47. Release the chains
48. Tripping
49. Corona
50. Ours till we catch them
51. Boy bye

52.	You have heard
54.	Using each other
55.	The puppy Ben
56.	It slipped
58.	We don't easily slip
60.	Who am I?
61.	Aloe
62.	Rat in the granary
64.	Man is a bedbug
69.	Wandering in the wild
70.	Possessed by the spirit of Manyuchi
73.	Chop the onions
74.	Cancer
75.	Blessed to be Vhudzijena's
76.	Child of my aunt
77.	Venus
78.	Cakes with no icing
80.	Elderly white man
82.	Beautiful just the way you are
84.	Letter to the girl child
86.	Craving for "mutakura"
88.	Flame Lily
89.	Loves and likes
90.	Friend
91.	Over the contour ridge
92.	Dolls and melons
94.	Willow tree
96.	Acquired through sweat
98.	Sleep paralysis
101.	Machonyonyo
102.	That which pleases daddy

103.	Condolences from the bewitcher
104.	Money back home
106.	Vandal
107.	"May I have it, I want it"
108.	I don't know you
110.	In the Lord's name
111.	You've gone Madhuve
112.	I have dug a little hole
113.	Premature baby
114.	Acting
116.	Player of the game
117.	Boundary crossing
118.	Springhare sort of sociopath
120.	Strength of a mad man
121.	We seem to …
122.	Question
123.	See you in heaven
124.	Root establishment
126.	Chitende
128.	*Uprooted interview*
134.	*Glossary of terms*
136.	*Shona names*
138.	*Names of places*
140.	*Shona euphemisms, idioms and metaphors ("EIM")*
145.	*Shona proverbs*

Introduction

A collection of poetry originally written in Shona by Samantha Rumbidzai Vazhure. "Zvadzugwa Musango" translates to "Those uprooted from their natural habitat" and explores the issues and celebrations of displaced immigrants and refugees living in the diaspora.

Samantha was born in the district of Barking and Dagenham (London, United Kingdom) in 1981, to Zimbabwean parents who were studying in the United Kingdom and returned to Zimbabwe a couple of years after independence. Samantha's father is of Karanga origin and her late mother was Zezuru. Samantha spent her childhood in Masvingo, Zimbabwe where she completed her education at Victoria Primary School and Victoria High Boarding School respectively. She returned to the United Kingdom in 1999 after completing her A levels. She studied Law and Business Administration at the University of Kent in Canterbury and proceeded to study a Postgraduate Diploma in European Politics, Business and Law at the University of Surrey. Samantha works as a financial services professional. She is married to her childhood sweetheart, and together they have two children.

Having lived in the UK for 20 years, Samantha felt inspired to write Shona poetry, not only to preserve and promote the Shona language and culture, but to encourage younger generations of immigrants to feel proud of who they are and where they are from. Having studied the Shona language, Literature in English and Divinity at A Level, Samantha has always felt compelled to write. The Karanga dialect is widely spoken in Masvingo, where Samantha grew up, and is unapologetically applied in her poetry. Issues explored through her poetry include equality, mental health challenges, abuse and toxicity in relationships, bullying and challenges of raising young families in the diaspora, to name but a few.

As she is bilingual, Samantha decided to translate her Shona poetry to English in order to share the Zimbabwean culture with the world, and to allow those who do not speak or understand Shona or the Karanga dialect to appreciate and learn from her poetry. It is worth noting that language translation carries with it cultural concepts that may not make sense at face value. The Shona language is rich in puns, idioms, metaphors and proverbs. As such, there are tools that will help to decode some unrelatable Shona traditional concepts the reader will come across in the poems. The concepts are italicised in the poems and defined at the back of this book.

Editor's note

When I was approached by the poet VaChifedza, Samantha Vazhure to edit her written verse, I was delighted to take on the task, assuming it would be a walk in the park. I believed the work would simply involve correcting minor errors, without realising that the job would affect me personally in the way it did.

The poetry in this collection is deep and will take you to long-forgotten places, times and memories; it will take you to times of joy and sadness, anger and much more. This poet uses poetic skill in a manner that will leave you educated and conscious, and sometimes introspecting about your own conduct with humanity.

As I read her poetry, I would break into laughter, and within a few moments of positive emotion I would be ravaged by sadness and compassion. That would sometimes be followed by feelings of anger, then I would find myself reflecting on my own conduct in my own home. I had not realised before that Shona poetry might have the ability to describe romance in a manner that would leave me beaming. One just has to read the poetry to understand where I'm coming from. When I read her feminist poetry, I found myself worrying for my own daughters, and hoping they would grow up conscious of male jackal behaviours out there. This book carries a thick, powerful voice in the arena of feminism and human equality. Samantha does not hesitate to speak her mind, which makes her poetry delightful. Although her poetry was written with Zimbabweans living in the diaspora in mind, it applies to most people globally.

Samantha's poetry is so diverse and varied, I found myself wondering how one person could articulate such a varied range of issues that affect humankind. Everyone who reads her poetry will be able to relate to some or all of it, and will at the very least have a few mind-expanding favourites.

I shall not take more of your time. I urge you to *cease measuring the snake with bark fibre,* this collection *is a feast for your eyes and your whole body.* Read this poetry in joy. I did my very best to *separate the grain from the chaff,* but if you come across a few stubborn grains, please try to chew them without breaking your teeth.

Daniel Mutendi

Acknowledgements

I would like to thank the following, who played a significant role in the production of this book:

Daniel Mutendi – Award-winning Shona novelist and translator who edited the original Shona poetry in Zvadzugwa Musango

DanTs Media – Book and cover design

My husband and children – for their unconditional love which encourages my creativity and; putting up with me when I selfishly turn into a hermit and escape into the world of writing

Friends and relatives – To all who do not get tired of cultivating my gift of writing

God – My heavenly father who strengthens and guides me in all I do, whose divine expressions flow through my gift of writing

*To my mother Hilary, whose cries went unheard ...
I finally found the voice that will end the suffering of women.
Your death forced me to grow and wake up. Rest in peace.*

To my grandmother Constance, who gave me the gift of language. Rest in peace.

To my daughter Hannah...you are precious, but no one is beneath you or above you.

Your Highness VaChifedza

You are acknowledged; gratitude *Masiziva*!
Empress *VaChifedza*!
The one with colossal breasts!
Daughter of King *Zengeya*
Save, the one from *Musikavanhu* in *Chipinge*
Who crossed *Tokwe* River on his way to *Chibi*
The last king of the *Ngowa* clan in *Chivi*
We appreciate you, your highness *VaChifedza*
First wife of *Tavengegwei*
Son of the wanderer with white canes!
Fierce woman whose bride price was a live warthog!
The *great agony aunt*!
Sister of *Kuvhirimara*, who relocated to *Mazvihwa*
Kuvhirimara, of the *Save* River, where girls like to play
An untouchable slippery eel
One you cannot fight with, lest you drown!
With skin like fabric of variegated patterns!

We are grateful!
For, *Kuvhirimira* who bore *Tinofa*
Tinofa bore *Chisanhu*, who fought the king's guard at *Mapanzure*
Chisanhu then bore *Chisiyawasiya*, a nomadic soul like *Jekanyika*
Nicknamed *Majange*, due to his greed for baby corn
Majange then bore *Musingawandi*, also known as *Chidhumbudede*
Chidhumbudede bore *Shanyurai*, whose English given name was Calvin
Shanyurai then bore *Shanyurai*, whose English given name was Charles
Shanyurai bore *Rumbidzai*, whose English given name was Samantha

She is here in me, Empress *VaChifedza*!
The one who carries enormous breasts!
Oh, hail *Maziziva*!
A beautiful ornament!
Venus who dwells near the sun!
The great aunt of aunts!
You are gratefully acknowledged!

"VaChifedza" is a title of respect for women of the fish totem. The original VaChifedza was a princess who married Tavengegwei of the lion totem, who in a coup took over as king from VaChifedza's father in Chivi. VaChifedza was known to have enormous breasts, which she threw over her shoulders to feed a baby she carried on her back. In this introductory praise poem, the poet traces her genealogy from the greatest female of the fish totem VaChifedza to the poet herself, who is also of the fish totem.

Uprooted

Ehuhuweee!
Hush now immigrant
You escaped war, hunger and troubles
From a country taken over by ruffians
You wander in pursuit of social welfare
You're a beautiful plant uprooted from nature
Whose purpose is to decorate a yard in a faraway land

Those uprooted from their natural habitat
Are important to keep homes adorned
But remember exotic plants need sunlight and water
And conditions mimicking what they are used to
Immigrant, stop your roots from drying out, do not wilt
Your migration would be pointless otherwise
Do not forget who you are, love yourself as you are
Maintain your ingenuity, take charge!
Stay alert to opportunities
Remember where you're from and know where you're going
We are one, God's creations are related and equal
You hurt anything, you hurt yourself
You harm others, you harm yourself
Don't fail love, simply love others as you love yourself
Those from where you're from and wherever you took refuge
Flush all forms of discrimination down the drain
Courage and gratitude are the hallmarks of love
Speak your mind, refuse to be silenced
But do not lie or feel shame, this bears no rewards
Appreciate the strength of words that escape your mouth
Think deeply before you wag your tongue
Natural wisdom and understanding, that is your intuition
You'll find will sharpen if you meditate
Your supernatural abilities will increase
When you get rid of the noise in your life
Because God speaks in a gentle whisper
That can only be heard by a selected few

Those uprooted from their natural habitat
Should be tough like an Aloe plant
Which survives for a very long time
Even during times of drought and famine
It maintains its medicinal potency
Which heals animals and sickly humans
Then when it is planted, in time
As if it was never uprooted
Quickly becomes grounded again

Ehuhuweee!
Hush now immigrant
You were uprooted but you will re-establish

The original poem, "Zvadzugwa musango" pacifies immigrants, encourages them to be resilient, not lose themselves and to remember who they are, and to stay grounded and balanced.

When will you return?

Child of my mother, where are you?
It's been too long, you may as well be a *Mujubeki*
You said you would return, but you're not back yet from Jo'burg
Where you're never seen, and you never phone
If only they had given you a visa to the Queen's nation
We would not be aching from this inoculation
You quit what you went to Jo'burg for, an education

Are you still alive my dear Chororo?

Come back home, hitch hike
Even if you ride on a haulage truck
On the day you return home, there'll be jubilation
We'll suffer from laryngitis due to avid ululation
For so many years our tears have incessantly flowed
Without you, life is bitter like a chicken's gallbladder
The gap you left in our family is a poison
That corrodes our minds, both the young and old
You yearned to be older, but fact is I'm older
As consecutive siblings we loved each other dearly
Although at times you could be a bit of a bully
Forcing me to chastise you like a delinquent
We however got on like darkness and candlelight
To me you were a treasured companion
Your absence aches like a worm beneath my skin

When mother died, I assumed you would return
When I got married, I hoped you would return
Telepathically, I invited you to my nuptials
Did you know our little brother tied the knot too?
He got married in Jo'burg where you are
Perhaps he hoped to hear you knocking on the door
Do you have a family of your own wherever you are?
I yearn to play my role of aunty to your children
I have children now, your niece and nephew
I'm always telling them about their dear uncle

As we gaze at the few old photographs of you
My high school sweetheart is your brother in law
He wishes to give you the acclamation of respect
"Thank you *Save!*" In homage and adulation

Do come and collect your share of my dowry
You two got along, come back to your mate
My mobile number remains the same for your sake
I hope you'll remember it and call in the end
I'm still holding on to your sweater
The one you gave me on the last day I saw you
I still have one of your paintings too

I hold onto memories of our childhood
I'll allow you to *pick the meat first* if you come back
You loved *chikangamwahama*; now you have forgotten us
Not a day goes by that I don't reminisce
The songs we listened to in joyfulness
And when we fought when you started it
Remember when I thrashed you with a cooking stick
Because you kicked my stomach during a karate match
I could have broken your back in half that day
Boy we had way too much energy back then
The memories sure are plenty

Remember the trouble we got into during holidays in *Chivi*?
Remember when I got lost whilst herding cattle?
After you coerced me to walk along a dry riverbed
Honestly that day you got me stressed out
Remember when we nearly dam-drowned in our DIY dish-boat?
Mbuya thoroughly trounced us and we swore to never do it again
Please come back, no questions asked
Past is past, we'll just look ahead

My heart aches for you
Come back *Musaigwa*, I won't fight with you
Come back *Dziva*, to play with me
No matter what, I'll always be proud of you
Child of my mother, come back please
Come even in a dream and tell me
Please do come and pacify me
I need to know, when will you return?

In the original rhyming poem "Unovuya riini?", the poet laments the disappearance of her brother, who after being denied a visa to join the rest of his family in the UK went to South Africa to study. After one year of studying, in August 2004, at the age of 20, the poet's brother Charles, nick-named "Chororo") informed the family by email that he had dropped out of college, was going to become an artist, would change his name and contact details, be out of touch for a while and would return home in December 2004. Charles never came back or got in touch.

Voice box

"Hey, zip it when grown-ups are talking!'
"Stand back, your noise is distracting!"
"What's wrong with you? You're just too wayward!"
"That child won't stop babbling away!"
"A proper calabash, the meowing cat of our nation!
Hold on adults, what are you playing at?
Can't you see? You've shut her voice box!

Hey hey we're in school now
"There's a question, give me an answer!"
All the boys throw their hands in the air
All the girls present a downward gaze
"What's the problem, where have the voices gone?"
Don't you remember? Her voice box was shut down!

"Who's howling in laughter over there?
Gosh, what a daughter in law he brought into the family
I bet we'll see a lot of drama this year
What's the problem over there? Be quiet Job's wife!
Sounds like a floozy flirting on a bus!
Your father in law can't stand the racket!"
But you are shutting down her voice box!

Hey hey, we're on the job now
"There's an issue that needs to be resolved"
Off to help the boss, see the men go
Off to cook at home, see the women rush off
"What's happening here women, are you inept?"
But can you not see? Her voice box is shut!

In the original poem "Gurokuro" the poet explores how discouragement of female children to express themselves freely (a common Zimbabwean cultural trait where society is often intimidated by confident women) ruins them for life. They grow up to become shy, fearful and timid, which may result in a sense of lacking a purpose in life.

My Lord

If you want me to address you as "My Lord"
You have to treat me like leopard hide
Behave like a grown man, not like a child
Drop the *miscellaneous* and philandering
You will see me beginning to trust you
Even my face will for you bear a smile
If you strengthen my heart like a stone
You will hear me moaning "*igwe*"

Drop your acts that make me suspicious
Stop running around like a horny stag
Dust off negativity like stale dandruff
Trust in me like a snuff calabash
Without annoying me like a dog tick
We will be together always like wild ducks
Always breaking into laughter
So in love, you and me

I am as gentle as a little lamb
My heart easily shreds to threads
Matters of the heart require emotional intellect
If you fail, words like daggers will fall on you
If you pass, I'll love you like a bullet fills a cartridge
And I'll be with you during tough times like illness
If you become competent at only these things
You will hear me calling you "My Lord!"

In the original rhyming poem "Shewe" the poet tackles a common hallowed title by which husbands of the older generation are addressed by their wives in Zimbabwe (the salutation is applied loosely too outside of marriage, by women to men of older generations). Men love to be adored, but sometimes they do nothing to deserve the adoration. The poet takes a feminist stance in this poem to advise men on attributes they might wish to display in order to earn some female respect. *Igwe is a title of respect and honour in Igboland (Nigeria).

Misfortune

Hello Queen Eliza, Knock! Knock! Knock!
Here we are in 2000, the world did not end
I'm the first in my neighbourhood to emigrate
I'm *feeling myself like honey*, you have no idea
So lucky to travel with no need for a visa, blessed Commonwealth!
Finally rode on a plane! I'm truly ecstatic
Why would I ever have needed to board one?
A sky hotel with bottomless toilets
I gormandise with pleasure as if I am in heaven
Literally devour everything, even things I do not recognise
Guzzle all sorts, both fizzy and alcoholic drinks
I'm overwhelmed with giddiness, Lord be with me
Travel opens eyes to new things, got to see for yourself
It has landed, the Candelabra of the clouds
Well done mesmerising hostesses, see you later
Those I've left back home, we'll see each other if God wishes
If it gets too exciting here, you will never see me there
Queuing up nicely, we wait for passport inspection
The biting cold reaches my marrow, and *asks what my totem is*
The bomber jacket, polyester tracksuit and viscose attire
Seem useless now, this common fashion from Edgars
In a stealth-like fashion, I hesitantly meander ahead
Repeating to myself the words I rehearsed
"Yes, I have some money
I've only come for a vacation
Someone is waiting for me outside"
My chest throbs hard like the band *Kutamburahuda*
My ancestors grace me, and I fluently *spit out English*
Get in! We're in! My passport has been stamped!
Soon as I pick up my large bag, I'm stopped again
All meat and fruit from my country goes straight into a bin
Made it through the needle eye, some passengers have been deported
Red phone, where are you? I look for it with red eyes
Ravhu, where on earth are you? You said you'd be dressed in red
I ring her number and all I hear is ngrrrrrrrr! ngrrrrrrr!
The phone is eventually switched off, proper dirt treatment
My belly is in distress, hunger will kill me today
Having sold my only cattle *Bhusvumani* and *Gwethlava*
I could only pay for the flight, and a red note remains
I wander around the airport and find nothing affordable

The note doesn't buy much, only a slice of cake and tea
Never go to places where your mother is not, I see red
I finally find a newspaper, and start researching ideas
Not much I can do with my remaining pound
Off to the trains, where I shall spend the night
Off I jump when I get booted out, and jump onto the next
Feels like I'm connecting buses at *Bhuka* bus station
Surviving on food remnants thrown away by others
On the third day, living on trains
Soon as I finish cursing my ancestors
I hear speakers of my language in my dialect!
They are from my hometown *children of my aunt*
By the end of the day, we were already grafting
My ancestors, thank you, for not forsaking me,
But never will I forget the day I saw misfortune

In the original poem "Ngwavaira" the poet assumes the persona of an immigrant who arrives in the UK as a visitor, with the intention to breach immigration laws by overstaying. The illegal immigrant arrives at the airport and the friend who is sponsoring the visit and supposed to pick them up from the airport does not turn up.

Adversity

It was the winter season
Living quietly in the Queen's nation
Still living illegally, still with no papers
Existing like a ghost, what could I do?
Very early in the morning, I returned from work
It was white with snow, which had fallen like an avalanche
Exhausted by my shift; "What kind of work is this?"
My micromanaging manager acts like a proper witch
Gulp, gulp! I drank my tea
As I faced much-needed sleep
Could never fall asleep with a frozen body
As I unwound in bed, I heard gu gu gu gu gu
The door was struck in police-like fashion
As I dragged myself out of bed, I reckoned
Must be the postman, who else could it be?
Through the peephole, my eye stuck out like a nail
Almost escaped its socket, couldn't believe what it saw
An army of policemen with guns and Alsatians
Oh my goodness, my intuition was spot on!
There are hundreds of them, this is the end of me
Did someone sell me out?
Enemy of progress, sociopath, who did this?
Deportation? You've got to be kidding me!
As I pondered my next move, they seemed to multiply
Covered in goosebumps, I stalked in reverse
Through the back window, I jumped out, very impressive!
Right into the fluffy snow, I thought "Catch me if you can!"
In Adam's style, I begged my feet to carry me
I propelled my strides like a thief in a ghetto location
My feet felt numb as if smeared by *Numb Location*
Hop over a fence, hop, hop, hop!
In the *kneeless people*'s gardens, on their tables
Hop, hop over neighbours' gardens, like stone river crossings
Cars full of police wailed in pursuit of me
By the strength of Samson, hop! Springing forward, hop!
Then I came to a road with a mass of people
Now I was whitebait amongst other small fishes
Head down, no gazing around
My huge head was mocked growing up, now a beacon
Police cars wailing everywhere, pee poo pee poo!

My only hope, my only wish, somewhere to hide…
Whitebait in lake *Kariba* looking for refuge…
My ancestors wondrously delivered me to my place of work
With feet long dead, in desperate need of a quilt
They were gobsmacked when I showed up in the ward
Their colleague in pyjamas on a shoeless body
"I was sleepwalking!"
A mad man's explanation; what could they do?
I made a call, "My neighbour, is the coast clear?"
Then she unravelled what had really happened
"The police were hunting down witnesses
A kid in the neighbourhood was stabbed"
A huge sigh of relief before I called a taxi
Then meditated in gratitude all the way home

In the original poem "Pfumvu" the poet impersonates an illegal immigrant who assumes they are subject to an immigration police inquisition, escapes their home through a back window, barefoot in the snow, and sprints back to work in their pyjamas to seek refuge.

Damn it!

I stand here proclaiming damn it!
I am screaming for a ticket
For liberty from oppressors
I mean the wearers of waistcoats
We feel intolerant of our tightening skirts
A scorching discomfort like wearing petticoats
Due to differences in our naughty bits
Treating us like tortoises, we did not ask for shells
We are nauseated by sexual harassment
They say, "love me first, you are chocolate"
Following those insults they pay us peanuts
The burden is as heavy as a haulage truck
If you persecute us, we'll launch a police docket
Let's move with the times and stop tip toeing
We want equality, hear us God damn it!

Relieve us from the burdens we carry
So heavy like rocks in pails
We want to escape these little confinements
Please grant us opportunities and rights
Parents if you want a large harvest
Or promising young girls who are independent
End child marriages and all cultural girl child calamities
Teach the little girls to cough out loud
To speak their minds to reveal what's in the folds of their hearts
To persist with reading and pursuing their education
And not to rush into marriage and having children
Encourage them to love themselves for who they are
Their bodies, spirits, minds and hearts
Oppressing us, and saying we don't think marrow-deep
We refuse it, we are wailing, please hear us!

Parents teach your male children
Mentor them into straightforward men
Mothers do the dishes with your sons
So they don't end up treating their wives like slaves
Counsel them about equality
Encourage them to say what's in their hearts
To avoid releasing tension by abusing their own children
Or verbally and physically abusing their wives
Some of them raping very little girls
We refuse it, we beg you, hear what we are saying!

Down with oppression of women
Down with abuse of women
Down with disrespect of women
Down with unequal treatment of women
Down with silo mentality amongst women
Down with domestic commotion
The likes of Takesure, sit down
Even you bosses at work, hold up
It is a lamentation, hear us, damn it!

Come on, let's go to war for equality
Men come along, you're part of the army
Can't win the war without you; we need you there
Soften your hearts, love is essential for this war
We are in a war of oppression
We are fed up, it's stifling
Seriously, please stop abusing us
Unchain our hearts and our voice boxes
I'm standing here blowing a loud trumpet
We no longer want chaos, let's remove these barriers
We've tampered with prickly pears, the glochids are killing us!
I've spread myself on the highway, must I die proclaiming damn it!

The original poem "Dhemeti" is a feminist lamentation for equality and unity, where the poet expresses exhaustion and discontent over practises that put women beneath men.

Mother's tongue

Children listen
Let us learn our mother's tongue
There's nothing special about batting your eyelids
Whilst you speak from the nose like little lambs
In a manner that your own mothers cannot hear

Start with vowels, A E I O U
Ba be bi bo bu
Ma me mi mo mu
Say *ona baba namai*
It's not difficult the mother tongue

Motsi, piri, tatu, ina, shanu
Tanhatu, nomwe, sere, pfumbamwe, gumi
This is how we count from one to ten
Give it a try, you can do it
Gumi neimwe comes after *gumi*

Muvhuro, Chipiri, Chitatu
China, Chishanu, Mugovera, Svondo
These are the days of the week
During the week, do you go to school?
At the weekend, do you go to worship?

Ndira, Kukadzi, Kurume
Kubvumbi, Chivabvu, Chikumi
Chikunguru, Nyamavhuvhu, Gunyana
Gumiguru, Mbudzi, Zvita
These are the names of months of the year

Matsutso, Chando, Chirimo, Zhezha
These are the seasons of the year
When it's the growing season do sow seeds?
Which is your favourite season?
My favourite is the summer

When you play, say "*dudu muduri*"
Or try "*ara uru, ara uru*"
These are the games from where we come
Come let us play *pada* and *chisveru*
Or let's play *chivande-vande* and be merry

In the original poem "Rurimi gwamai" the poet encourages subsequent generations of immigrants to learn basic words and numbers in their mother language, to learn basic terms, such as months and seasons, and to explore games and activities from their country of origin. This basic exposure helps to provide a sense of belonging and grounding, which may minimise the impact of identity crisis.

Apparitions

They look at us foreigners like chicken droppings
And they treat us just like the chaff of grain
We're exhausted by it; our energy is depleted
Ashamed of who we are, as if we're dim-witted

Back home our own people see us as apparitions
If you don't have money, don't bother returning
We no longer feel free or welcome there
Even if they drug us with tototo

Our hunger yearns for peanut butter relish
But it's unpalatable, our palates are seared
Our hearts are constricted by a barricade
With nowhere to call home, we are apparitions

In the original poem "Magoritoto" the poet explores a predicament most immigrants living in the diaspora face - they feel like they don't belong back home or in the country in which they reside.

MaTanzaniya

I give up on the chores in this house
I do not recall the last time I played with soap
I clench my jaw as I reminisce about Gloria
She helped to look after my kids the other year
Dear Father hear me, for I'm a believer
The man in this home if forever drunk
He's exasperated by a job that assaults him
Even in my job, they drive me with a whistle
Our children are sad due to soulless parents
Their mother and father are forever silent
Joy escaped our home, what do we do?

Rats are rampant, we dodge them everywhere
A spiritual affliction, they don't touch poison
If they were mice, we'd catch and roast them
My home is colonised by MaTanzaniya

In the original poem "MaTanzaniya", the poet describes a rat infestation, as a result of neglect and loss of control. The poem is an allegory of a life encapsulated with negative energy. "MaTanzaniya" are a species of large rats that once infested Zimbabwe and were thought to have been introduced by haulage trucks that transported goods from Tanzania to Zimbabwe.

Prisoner of stuff

Liberty is not freedom!

If you free yourself from poverty back home
And find a new life of abundance
Then become addicted to stuff
You are a prisoner
You are essentially fettered
You are still being controlled

You have no liberty!

In the original poem "Nhapqwa yezvinhu" the poet advises that liberty comes from a detachment from stuff (material things) and a life without addictions.

Ego

You will never know your life purpose
Until you *dig a little hole* and discard your ego in it
You do not know the intention of your existence
Until you remove the jacket you're wearing, ego
An infirmity devastating the whole world
All you have, all your achievements
What other people think of you
Selfishness, self-absorption
Avoidance of piety
These are some of the snags of ego
Let go of these things, that's your ego
Discard these and discover your life purpose.

In the original poem "Chikurira" the poet suggests that letting go of one's ego is one of the best ways to discover life's intention and one's purpose in life.

Evil spirit

Have you ever wondered
What an evil spirit is?
    Do you remember the phenomenon?
    That took place when you went to the bush
You shat your heart out and left the dirt inside!
Now you are full of shit ...
    Dirt now drips into your mind
    The stink diffuses into your behaviour
Evil is all we can smell
Show us where you buried your heart!
We might find it before it rots!
    We'll crack open your chest and put it back!
    So you can put to rest your evil spirit!

In the original poem "Mweya wesvina" which means either "evil spirit" or "smell of dirt", the poet interchanges these meanings to highlight that even the cruellest people can find their hearts and end their evil behaviour.

Take this needle

Oi! Oi! You! Take this needle!
You split my heart in half
You do not seem to harbour a heart
You truly treat me like your rival

Hold it carefully do not drop it
You expertly harmed my emotions
I am exhausted of putting on a brave face
I literary carry around an apprehensive look

I was asleep but am awake now
But I am not gifted with the skill of cursing
To hell with your pointless unreasonable expectations
I will make sure of your government's dissolution

You act like you have changed, that is why I am still here
But the reality is my heart is no longer here
As such my darling, here is the deal
Mend my heart quickly, do not dilly-dally

I do not want to see any visible patches
Tighten the stitches, do not leave it hanging loose
Forget your need to be adored, you are not a hero
Do not test me, you will cause me bad karma

Sew my heart up triple times
When you are done please rinse out my rage
Leave it clean and white like *sosoti* berries
Oi! Oi! You! Take this needle!

In the original poem "Gashirayi nareti!" the poet assumes the persona of a woman fed up of subtle and hidden abusive tendencies, and encourages the perpetrator who seems to have improved but often slips back to his old ways, that the only reason she is still in the relationship is for him to proactively mend her broken heart and not to cause further damage.

Dare me!

It's me *Masiziva*, disturber of offenders
I was asleep, but now speak consciously
Just thought to tip you off, before we go any further
This time I have not named and shamed, I've been kind
But to those who carry on mischievously
And repeat offenders who I've pardoned previously
I will dry you outside the way we dry chaumoulier
Especially the egotists, you're easier to pique
Yes you, the abusers and drama mongers
You don't listen, but you've been warned
Those with ears have heard
Dare me!

In the original poem, "Itii pqwe" the poet uses a common Shona expression as a warning that she is on the brink of naming and shaming repeat abusers and offenders.

Morningstar

I know, no two days are alike
Perhaps you're late due to overtime
But soon as it clocks nine at night time
Without a call or you returning home
You must be out there hunting for punani
Especially because you left wearing denims
I told you off before for your taste in fashion
And I thrashed you before with a monkey wrench
When I caught you standing and chatting with *Koni*
And when you arrived late after partying with *Thulani*
I had to stop when you called the police on me
It was rather painful though, was it not?
When I kicked you around screaming, "*Kamani!*"
You crying as if troubled by onion juice
I have warned you before to distance yourself from pussy
You don't get tired of looking for mistresses
When you're not with them they're with younger boys
Are you looking for disease to bring back home?
I do not want a life of juggling prescriptions
Why on earth do you not listen boy?
Before the cock crows in the morning
When you finally get home in the morning
I'll be waiting for you, wielding a Morningstar.

The original rhyming poem, "Nyeredzi yamangwanani" (a spiked ball medieval weapon) raises awareness of the abuse of men by women in relationships, a growing trend in the diaspora.

Bones

Nothing hurts my heart more
Nor throbs my head more
Than one who leaves meat on bone
Thought to vent this in a poem
That when I find meat on bone
I subscribe to a labour of love
It may be chicken at Nando's
Served with peri chips
Please do not be envious
It is a gastronomic war
When I roast it in cast-iron
Or grill it on the BBQ
Different varieties of meat…
I'm not fussy about the nicks
As long as it's on bone
If it's stewed all day
Overcooked and falling apart
Served with potatoes
Children raised here do not know hunger
They gnaw the meat like lazy crows
Feeding on a carcass in the wild
They play with meat like little monkeys
That overturned the grill plate
On a fire left unmanned
By one who had to rush to the bush
Never mind I'm only tripping
About those who leave meat on bone

"Makodo" is the original rhyming nonsense verse in which the poet expresses her love for meat on bone.

Messengers

Every being on earth is a messenger
Commissioned to a specific purpose
Even those with disturbing behaviour
Are under divine commission
Do not waste time worrying about them
All of this is intended and predestined
Learn to forgive those who do you wrong
All they are doing is playing their role
This does not mean you forget their wrongs
Everything truly happens for a reason
Even the strangest and most ridiculous
Could be family, friends or your enemies
Even you are an appointed messenger
Your role is to learn your true purpose
If you do not perform your intended role
Darkness will haunt you until you learn it
It was all predetermined, no point fighting it
Soften your heart, use your free will
The greatest thing in all you do, is love
Be mindful of this to fulfil your purpose
We are one, all messengers of the Creator

In the original poem "Vatumwa" the poet explores the metaphysical subject of oneness, synchronicity, purpose of life and being connected to the Source of all energy, God.

Jackal

There's a man, a real jackal
Today he's resentful towards his Missus
Tomorrow he elevates and treats her like a tutee
Must be borderline, behaving like an untrained bull
Binges on aphrodisiacs, you know, *Mugondorosi*!
Leaving his wife untouched as if she has no tushie
Darkening her heart like the water in river *Mukuvisi*
Does he not know that the yoni is divine?
Day after day he's fed barley thick porridge
Served with grilled home-made boerewors
And treated to handpicked mulberries
Then he has his dirty overalls laundered
But like a two-headed snake, he cannot focus
Addicted to the chalice, he's a real jackass
His behaviour resembles the stench of mouldy socks
His sociopathic behaviour is truly diabolic
Today he cries out loud upon the mention of divorce
Tomorrow he says he's not interested in the Missus
He sparks an itch like the Chickenpox
Our faces scrunch up like we're chewing bitter pills
Can somebody please put him on a training course?
Where he can learn to treat this Venus like a queen
Before we chuck him into *Tokwe Mukosi*

The original rhyming poem "Jakarasi" describes men with jackal tendencies; cunning, opportunistic predators that are difficult to trust.

Release the chains

Your mind is a prison
Barricading your way like spokes
Clenching your feet like compression socks

Pay attention, I am your teacher
Preaching what your preacher won't teach you
Sharpen your ears, or you might miss the point

Only you can release the shackles
You can unlock the chains that gaol you
Do so by scrutinising your mind

Do you love yourself truly?
This is your life purpose
And worry not what others think

Know that mistakes are common
If you fail, you're still human
Stop being too eager to please

Let go of whatever hinders your progress
Erase thoughts that leave you feeling helpless
Like being brought up to think you're useless

Have some self-respect
Bitter pills have blessed effects
There is nothing else, don't self-neglect

The only thing tying you down are chains
A negative energy that seems devilish
They're all in your head, they're imaginary chains

You can do it, release the chains!

The original poem "Sunungura ngetani" presents the idea that freedom is in your mind and only you can unchain it. Once you free your mind, you will live a life full of joy.

Tripping

She stuffs her lips into her nose
Something tripped her, it must be him
Don't start with her, when she fumes
When she grafts, as though possessed

She cinches her waist, exhausted
He has already prepared a snare
"Have a bath my queen, and I'll rub your back"
"Yes *Shewe, your words are in my ears*"

He clutches the bottle of oil, as if in love
"Lie down, and I'll rub down your body pain"
He kneads and strokes her, as if he cares
He climbs on her back, so as to reach

Somewhat later, he too is tripped
And falls and sinks into the honey pot
Made it through the rear door, what does it matter?
She releases her tension, as if she never tripped

That's how they're tripped up, in their own homes

In the original poem "Kugumburana" (which means "upsetting each other" or "tripping"), the poet interchanges these meanings to explore a common method of making up in romantic relationships when couples are mad at each other.

Corona

If you suck it up on the cross
Without changing whatsoever
You will not be awarded a corona

You will be busted
Your mind twisted
You will end up in a ditch

A holy habit cleanses not a foul soul
A bone containing no marrow easily crushes
They who diligently seek, find

So if you suck it up; in trauma
Whilst making positive changes
You may eventually earn the corona

There is a Zimbabwean religious hymn which encourages sucking up to adversities on the cross (like Jesus) until you're awarded a corona. In the original poem "Korona" the poet advises that situations do not change unless you take active steps to change, especially in abusive situations.

Ours till we catch them

Bestow upon them their human rights
Leave judgement to He who created them
Liberate them in order to liberate us
So they may stop lying to us day after day
So they may stop abusing us in relationships

They make great effort, they really do
Do they not want to be loved and to have families?
But they pretend to love us, we can see this
We're in a Gehenna, we're all dying here
Disingenuous love leads to emotional abuse

They are prisoners in marriages
Imprisoned by a sham life imposed on them
They are suffocated by our bedding
And starve us of sex, violating our human rights
Making us feel like we are dry and useless

They are in our lives, our homes are full of them
They verbally, emotionally and physically abuse us
We know for now they are ours, they have no choice
They lie to us, but we can see through it all
Until the day we catch them at it, of course

In the original poem "Ndedzedu kusvika tadzibata" the poet pleads with the powers that be, to liberate gays and lesbians, recognise they are human and leave judgement to the One who created them. The original poem deliberately omits the noun "ngochani" used in Shona to identify gays and lesbians, because gays and lesbians find the term derogatory. Due to lack of gay rights in Zimbabwe, a lot of gays and lesbians find themselves in mixed orientation relationships, where they inadvertently emotionally abuse their partners, due to long term frustrations with regards to their sexual identity.

Boy bye

If my liberty
Intimidates you

If my confidence and belief in myself
Give you a headache

See you later little man!
I mean boy bye!

I'm a woman
I am joy
If you don't get that
You're foolish
You're a kid
A failure!

I'm an entity and not an extension
Don't try to rain on my parade

If you try to hurt and bring me down
I'll give you the middle finger

See you later little man!
I mean boy bye!

The original poem "Tovonana chikomana" is a self-empowerment poem for women who have to deal with men who feel threatened and don't know how to relate to confident strong women.

You have heard

The child expert is the one who is childless
Here in the diaspora parents have a problem
There are laws that rebuke child rearing
The sort of child raising that we experienced
Such as the trouncing of buttocks
Which we were quite numb to
But now all we can do is caution, gently
With that eye that says, "you have heard!"

Have you bathed my friend?
"It's too cold I'm not bathing today mum"
Have you read today my child?
"I've got a headache today mum"
Have you been outside to exercise?
"Nah, the tv is the real deal"
Have you made your bed?
"Is it not I who sleeps on it?"
Oh hell no, I am *Masiziva*, no child talks to me like that
Not the one I gave birth to, I say hell no!
When they become too provocative
I engage my talking eye that says, "You have heard!"

The goat herder is given the ears
How then do we open the ears?
Of those whose ears we cannot twist
How do we counsel these sisters?
Growing up in a land full of governesses
How do we teach these sons of ours?
Growing up where children cannot be beaten
Pinching or whipping, not here parents, we don't
Restrict what they love, so they see we mean business
Nurture more, quit intransigence, we don't do whips here
With these few words, you have heard!

In the original poem "Kuzvihwa wazvihwa" the poet explores the challenges of disciplining children in the diaspora, using methods that are non-abusive and compliant with the law. The issue is viewed as a challenge by most African parents living in the diaspora, because they were raised by the hand (i.e. use of corporal punishment) and this is the most natural way they know to instil discipline. The poet advises holding back from corporal punishment and nurturing children instead.

Using each other

"All she wants are my papers"
"Give me your papers and I'll be your slave"

This is the unwritten agreement
Of those entering sham marriages
That tie hearts up in thistle

An existence of imprisonment
Twisting and turning each other's heads
Children of the same country treating each other like mops
Due to the scarcity of legal immigration status

You, the slave ...
You are sex starved
Your money is taken from you
Love is withheld daily from you
What can you do, you need papers, right?

You, holder of papers ...
Find one who needs nothing from you
To dissipate your fear of being used
One you can love wholeheartedly
So you can enjoy the taste of real love
Our days here on earth are finite

In the face of dire need, a lion preys on a tortoise
If you know you're using each other
In a manner that requires living together
Why don't you just love each other truly?

The original poem "Kuitisana" explores visa dependency abuse.

The puppy Ben

Ey ma'am
Whose child are you embracing?

Gosh, if it isn't the little boy Ben!
The friend of your daughter Gwen
Child of yesterday Ben
A little Ben Ten
You really are training him to be a dog
His mother will *eat a dog*
What if you infect him with disease?
Or you might catch a geriatric pregnancy?
You should be ashamed ma'am
Allow Ben to grow ma'am
You are disturbing man
Your behaviour is foul
Please release Ben!

The puppy Ben

The original poem, "Mbgwanana Bhen", rebukes the predatory behaviour of older women targeting men young enough to be their sons, for love affairs.

It slipped

For many days we have come together
Cold weather demands carnal convergence
Result! A seed is eventually sown
I perceive odours and spend all days asleep

Thank you, Father, for answering my prayers
Morale is high in our family, there's no more drama
We now await the nine months
To be united with our child

Congratulations! Congratulations! The world celebrates
Hoorah! Our Father has been good to us
Those who knit and crochet, please launch the graft
Those who can't, off you go to Mothercare

As the months progress the baby kicks
It's pretty skilful, I'm certain it's content
When it goes quiet, I drink ice cold water
After a while, it kicks again and I'm jubilant

A midnight startle, I feel damp warmth
A touch down below reveals a bloody puddle
Father if you have taken it, what a punishment
I begin a lamentation, I can see no longer

On arrival at the hospital, we beg for help
"We're afraid there's not much we can do
If you're miscarrying, it can't be helped
Pray if you may, it might just stop"

The days have progressed, my cervix dilates
They listen for a heartbeat, and confirm there's nothing
The labour pains begin, with nothing to look forward to
Push baby girl, push; push out the body of your child

It has come out, a little boy
Looks so healthy, looks like his father
Why have you chastised us with such a whip Father?
What do we do now? All we have are tears!

On arrival at home, all we see is darkness
Shall we start all over? This is depressing!
God dry our tears, our eyes are blinded
It had progressed so well, but the pregnancy slipped

The original poem "Yasvotoka" is about miscarriage and the emotional turmoil it brings.

We don't easily slip

Phone rings, "Mum come and get me!"
What is going on, I've only just dropped you?
"The whites have started, they tripped me, and I fell!"
No, my child, you will stay in school
If I come to get you, we've accepted to fall
Remain steadfast, we don't easily slip

Sat at the table, I see tears falling
What is wrong, you were happy just now?
"The whites are at it again; one pointed a knife at me
They say my skin is too dark, it contaminates the school!"
No, my child; weeping solves nothing
Tomorrow I will go to your school
And speak to the head to sort this out
Remain steadfast, we don't easily slip

"Mum I'm ill today, I can't go to school"
What is your ailment, shall we go to hospital?
"My disease is terminal, I am different
The disease is my skin, how do I heal from this?"
Listen child, and let my words sink
You are beautiful just the way you are
You will go to school and learn all you can
They want you to lurk behind, and to that, I say "NO!"
Remain steadfast, we don't easily slip

"Park your car further away when you pick me up
I would rather ride my bike than to be up picked by car"
Why? You want to walk for miles in this freezing cold?
"They say we are thieves; blacks can't afford your car"
Now listen child, to the words of your mother
Them saying we steal is simply projection; they stole from us
We are in this country to take back our wealth
We are going nowhere, this is our home
Remain steadfast, we don't easily slip

The original poem "Hatitsvedzi zvokumanya" explores the challenges presented by racially inspired bullying in schools. The poet encourages calling it out and never giving up on fighting it.

Who am I?

My body is a coat
That I put on the day of my birth
And take off on the day of my death
The one I see in the mirror is not me
So who am I then?

All I have may be taken
My achievements may be superseded
What I'm proud of may disappear
These things do not define me
So who am I then?

I was created in the image of the Creator
The Creator is a spirit, everyone is a spirit
Worldly things are finite, even the body rots
But the spirit has no beginning nor end
The one in the mirror perishes
The one with things perishes
I look after my spirit
For I am a spirit

The original poem "Umbori ani" is a metaphysical poem exploring who we are.

Aloe

The beauty of an Aloe in undebatable
It adorns a yard with its wonderful flowers
Bees and insects love to play on it
Ruminants and other animals feed on it
The value of an Aloe is undebatable

The strength of an Aloe is indisputable
It heals when consumed
Even sick chickens heal from it
It will gently soothe burns and bites
The value of an Aloe is indisputable

The resilience of an Aloe is irrefutable
During times of drought, it remains resolute
When it rains its flowers will sprout
If you forget it, it will not forget you
The value of an Aloe is irrefutable

The original poem "Gavakava" appreciates the beauty and usefulness of an Aloe plant.

Rat in the granary

Thought I'd return a favour
We shared your tinned beef in boarding
When I heard you were here, I was elated
And asked you to pay me a visit
Thinking you were still human
Not knowing you had become rabid
You arrived at the station without a bag
Assuming it was a day visit, I dismissed the clue
After a week, you were still lurking
Recruitment agencies were quiet
Yet you arrived empty handed
You didn't think to bring underwear
After a while you decided to illuminate
That you burnt bridges with your own family
I empathised, thinking you were still human
You misused my phone, hunting for toy boys
Took my special clothes and used them as pyjamas
Took my papers and used them to look for work
When you got paid, you didn't bother helping me
You bought junk food, trinkets and useless stuff
Have you not heard of contributions?
Do you know what a budget is?
Misused my oils as if you watered the garden with them
Rearranged my photographs and decor
But without tidying or cleaning up your mess
Judging and probing me as if you were in your own house
Gormandising my food like a rat in a granary
Skipped doing the dishes, made me your slave
I tried to tell you that *only sunshine is free*
But two months in I'd had enough of your nonsense
Having to put up with your daily erratic moods
Our friendship thinned due to your antisocial behaviour
Because your persona became unbearable
But as we know, *every sin has a bitter end*
One day when you stepped out, I liberated myself
You found me gone, and I left you in the granary

The original poem "Gozho mudura" is about a visit from an old friend from back home who knows no boundaries and overstays their welcome.

Man is a bedbug

They sang at a wedding
The elderly women of *Chivi*
"Man is a bedbug! Man is a bedbug!
Seeeee yooouuuuu when you're in tatttteeerrrrssss!
Sister-in-law please take the baby so I can cook
Hell no, that ain't my problem
Sister-in-law please take the child so I can toil the field
Hell no, that ain't my problem
Seeeee yooouuuuu when you're in tatttteeerrrrssss!"

Today they find her ravaged and exhausted
By the bed bug she found for herself
She's *being bitten by the thing she dug up herself*

Bedbug!
It first drowns you in love
Then licks you all over like honey
It'll treat you like a queen
Whilst constructing its way to your heart
When it enters your bloodstream
It will begin its real task
Biting you in the dark
And shying away in the light

Bedbug!
Clever like a sable antelope
And painful like measles
Scandalous, disgraceful, nefarious
Leaves the life of a woman in fog

Makes a woman give up her career
Then does not give her money
Then is always mad at her
And will cheat on her with her family
With no ounce of shame
Even with the respectable, it'll not stall to flirt
Even within its profession, it *can't get out of dresses*

Even on public transport, it winks at blushing flirts
Yet it's a fool with no real strength
Leaves a woman discontented
Her vulva is forever pulsating
Look at her now she's putting on weight
Bedbug created a binger who eats for comfort
An impotent husband is constantly annoyed
By the face of the wife he married
VaKaranga please find it *Chipikiri*!
VaZezuru please hand it *Mugondorosi*!
VaRozvi please give it *Muchemedzambuya*!

Bedbug!
It's given children
Then it's disgusted by her
Then stops her breastfeeding
Because it won't share her breasts
Mama's boy should go back to its mama!

It'll say you're too fat
Or that you're too thin
Humiliates a woman
And yells at a woman

It will put a woman down
It will beat up a woman
And abuse her physically and emotionally
It's jealous of its own children
It will separate her from friends
And even her relatives
It competes with her
Withdraws sex from her
Or even rapes her!
It blames her for everything
Never takes responsibility for its actions
Never offers to help her
Patronises a woman
Punishes a woman
Controls a woman

It remains ungrateful when she prepares a feast
Even if she's a perfect woman
A Proverbs thirty-one woman
Even when she makes the home opulent
You will hear it whinging ceaselessly
"You treat me like a dog, yet I'm a king;
You're useless, unlike so and so"

Its mobile phone is forever clenched
Its heart by harlots is forever clenched
Wife wishes she could cut it up with a machete
Why doesn't it tell her what she's doing wrong?
So moody it can't possibly be bothered with that
Why not give her the *divorce token payment*?
Then it changes and begins to love her again
Today is delightful
Tomorrow is painful
Today it says you had it coming
Tomorrow it says it's sorry
Today it tickles
Tomorrow it's bitter
A proper whirlwind
Makes your head spin
Ravages and ravages
Until you lose sanity
You'll never know where you stand
Marriage to it is a Gehenna
Because of the bedbug living off her blood

Sucked until you lose your sense of self
Sucked until you coagulate
Energy depleted till you long for death
Endless, continuous blood suction
The bedbug's thirst is unquenchable

It's addictive, you can't leave
Who do you tell?
They tell you *"groan in situ"*
Our proverb does teach
"A wife bravely bears all nagging from her husband"

But why can't this bed bug be plucked off?
It could be due to our own burdensome proverb
"Domestic frictions strengthen domestic living"

Then there's hope
Hope for love
Hope for happiness
Hope for a complete man
Hope that the abuse will end
Hope like gambling is addictive
Hope
It's only hope
Then there's hope

Her head pounds
Intestines are tangled
Feet swollen
Head is bald
Eyes bloodshot
Face infested with spots
Even her bits have disappeared
The flesh gives up
The soul is letting go

As you lay on your deathbed
Waiting for the moment
You face the shadow of the valley of death
There comes the light that marks the end
You are dying girl child
On your way to your grave
Then you remember *Manyuchi's* words
To her bed bug Jay Z

"So what are you gonna say at my funeral
Now that you've killed me?
Here lies the body of the love of my life
Whose heart I broke
Without a gun to my head
Here lies the mother of my children
Both living and dead
Rest in peace my true love

Who I took for granted
Most bomb pussy
Who because of me sleep evaded
Her shroud is loneliness
Her God was listening
Her heaven will be a love without betrayal
Ashes to ashes
Dust to side chicks."

The original poem "Murume itsikidzi" raises awareness of emotional, verbal and physical abuse of women in marriage and romantic relationships, usually inflicted by men with narcissistic, misogynistic and sociopathic tendencies. Sadly, most women cannot speak up or recognise abusive behaviours due to their individual upbringing, culture and other reasons. If left unresolved, abuse may result in illness, which may be fatal. Quoted words in the final stanza are lyrics directly translated from Beyoncé Knowles "Lemonade" album (Poem: Apathy, written by Warsan Shire), in accordance with the CMSI Code of Best Practices in Fair Use for Poetry. NB. Beyoncé's name is translated to "Manyuchi" by the poet, a befitting praise name illustrating that Beyoncé is Queen Bey (bee), a female icon who empowers other women.

Wandering in the wild

Ey you, whose child are you?
I'm a child of my family, but
I was sold to those who paid my dowry
I'm wandering in the wild

Ey you, where are you from?
I was born in England, but
I grew up in Zimbabwe
I'm wandering in the wild

Ey you, which is your family?
I have my siblings, but
I also have a husband and children
I'm wandering in the wild

Ey you, where do you work?
I run my own company, but
I work with several clients in various offices
I'm wandering in the wild

Ey you, which church do you belong to?
I was baptised by the Dutch Reformed, and grew up Methodist
I wed in the Catholic church; I was wandering in the wild ...
But I belong to God

The original poem "Musango ndodzungaira" is an example of an identity crisis.

Possessed by the spirit of Manyuchi

I am a good girl, me
Well mannered
Well raised
Competent
But...

We all get tired
Pressing on is not easy
It is roofs that conceal domestic squabbles
These homes are full of idiots and prats!

I am still young and feisty
So when my wounds are tampered with
I mean the oozing lesions of love
I become possessed by the spirit of *Manyuchi*!

When I'm fed up
I'm possessed by the bee sting spirit

I find myself in *Manyuchi*'s beehive
        Patron of women going through fuckery!

        "What's worse, lookin' jealous or crazy?
Jealous or crazy?
I'd rather be crazy!"

                                Mscheeew!
                            Don't touch me
                          Don't speak to me
                           Don't look at me
                       Stay away from me
                                    Don't...

N'iiiiiiiiiiiiiiiiiiiiiiiiiiiiiiiiiiiiiiiii   N'a!
    Sting!
    Aaaaaaaaaaaaaarrrrrrrrrrgggggghhhhhh!!!

Nah nah! Hell nah!
    "Sorry, I ain't sorry"

        Oops, looks like I iron-scorched your pants
        Oops, looks like I burnt your favourite meat
        Oops, I stepped on your phone by accident!
        Oops, your recorded tv programs deleted themselves!

    "When you hurt me, you hurt yourself, don't hurt yourself"
"When you diss me, you diss yourself, don't hurt yourself"
"When you love me, you love yourself"

N'iiiiiiiiiiiiiiiiiiiiiiiiiiiiiiiiiiiiiiiii   N'a!
    Sting!
    Aaaaaaaaaaaaaarrrrrrrrrrgggggghhhhhh!!!

Nah nah! Hell nah!
    "Sorry, I ain't sorry"

        Beans on toast today!
        No bean for you tonight!
        Don't get to touch my coochie!
        Ain't bathing you tonight!

"When you hurt me, you hurt yourself, don't hurt yourself"
"When you diss me, you diss yourself, don't hurt yourself"
"When you love me, you love yourself"

And now, as we lay our heads to sleep…
(A whisper… a whisper)

"Just give my fat ass a big kiss boy"

"I got hot sauce in my bag, swag…"

If you want to kiss it better
Hit me with a whip!
"I'd rather be crazy"

Goddang, bring the whip!

The original poem "Dhinhiwe shavi raManyuchi" is about a disgruntled, passive aggressive wife being driven crazy in an emotionally abusive relationship in which she chooses to remain. She vents but eventually opens up to a kinky night of making up, as is common in a cycle of abuse. Quoted words are lyrics directly translated from Beyoncé Knowles "Lemonade" album (songs: Hold up; Don't hurt yourself; Sorry), in accordance with the CMSI Code of Best Practices in Fair Use for Poetry. NB. Beyoncé's name is translated to "Manyuchi" by the poet, a befitting praise name illustrating that Beyoncé is Queen Bey (bee), a female icon who empowers other women.

Chop the onions

Diaspora is an equaliser
Women, men, the rich and the poor
You all have to chop the onions
Marriage is for equals; this requires no testimony
There are no aunts here to act as mediators

What's wrong men, you seem to have teary eyes?
Or is it the onions making your eyes water?
Or is it that you really hate doing chores?
What do we do then, there are no maids here?
You better help women to ease domestic squabbles

We are not back home where you never help women
We all go to work and return exhausted
If you find yourself not helping, you're an offender
You women, learn to show appreciation when you get help
If you do this, you will find peace like gazing at stars

Before you go out, men, do some tidying up
Do it with a smile, no need to scrunch up your face
Don't sit there, not helping, just 'cause you gave my father cows
Come on, get up and chop the onions
Do it quick, *whilst the donkeys are braying*

The original poem "Chekai hanyanisi" encourages men to pull their weight and help women with chores or otherwise in the home.

Cancer

The diagnosis is malignant
I do not mean opportunistic Ivy
That spreads on other trees until it drops them
I mean cancer, a disease that spreads like spilled water

Affliction of cancer
A war in your body that is quite intense
Humankind is on the brink of obliteration
A dreadful disease that slithers on you
We are being destroyed by cancer
Women, men, boys and girls
It is not selective, it takes kids and the elderly
It carefully selects where it will land
Usually when you least expect it
It is shockingly atrocious
Like pumpkin leaves, it spreads everywhere
Usually it's exposed when ripe and too late
If you used to be proud, walking with your head up
The misfortune of cancer will force your head down

Cancer is a teacher with lessons to be learnt
In your body there's a war spreading
Like a government dispersing its propaganda
Cease the war before it goes too far
There's a lesson here so lend me your ears
Use your freewill, your soul craves authenticity
And refuse to be ruled by this deadly illness

Live a genuine life
Relish life and live freely
Go against these codes and you will perish
It is a deadly disease, the scourge of cancer

The original poem "Gomarara" is about the ruthlessness of cancer, and how living a stressful and inauthentic life may exacerbate the viciousness of the scourge.

Blessed to be Vhudzijena's

It is I *Masiziva* with enormous breasts
I'm loved by *Makwiramiti*, I struck gold
It is I *Masiziva*, daughter of *Musaigwa*
Fortune certainly smiled on me
I was chosen by *Vhudzijena*

Hurrah! Hurrah! All *those long baths paid off*
Let's move onward *Soko*, stop scratching in rumination
So long VaKaranga, I have found the one who loves me
Hurrah! *Mukanya*, my one and only *Soko*

He *thrives on thievery*
Now *Makwiramiti* has pilfered my heart
After a moderate time, *Pfumojena* begins
And says "Empress *VaChifedza* you're a bit crazy
I'm leaving for fun elsewhere, so stay; I'll be back *Masiziva*"

Oh my days, does he not know who I am?
Princess *Masiziva* from the *Musaigwa* clan!
Soko, do not fight with water, or you will drown
He says "We are from *Matonjeni*, we are the rainmakers!
But *your words are in my ears,* my Empress *VaChifedza*
I will not fight with you"

Mukanya proudly wanders back home
Hurrah! My madness has paid off
I am truly blessed
To be loved by *Vhudzijena*

In the original praise poem for her husband, "Ndapinda machena naVhudzijena" (Vhudzijena being a male of the Monkey totem) the poet illustrates that no marriage is perfect, but true love, communication and compromise are tools proven to make it work.

Child of my aunt

He arrives in the land of those *with no knees*
Child of my aunt, give him a round of applause!
For running away from problems in *Gwitima*
He freezes to death and has become moody
He has become a coward possessed by laziness

"Sit down and read books, upskill yourself
Catch my underwear, it needs washing
Take my headwrap, I want *sadza* ready by the time I get back!"
He crawls to wash up, and when he's done he gets cooking
He groans as he contemplates, "peace and joy where are you?"

Momentarily he declares "I'm stepping out
You stay home while I catch a breath of fresh air."
He escapes and off he goesssssssssssssssss!
He finds friends and with them begins shenanigans
A coward now possessed by indolence

There he goes and *can't get out of dresses*
Drunk and befuddled, he forgets his true purpose
Hey *child of my aunt* wake up, you will be abandoned
You better read books so you can be like the *kneeless ones*
We'll celebrate, when *he who used to eat dry starch eats it with meat*!

In the original rhyming poem "Gwana gwavatete" (which in the Karanga dialect is a term used to describe anyone from the Masvingo province, where it is presumed everyone from there is in some way related), the poet explores how easily displacement can affect relationships and our true selves. In the context of this poem, every foreigner is related due to common struggles shared in the diaspora.

Venus

In English they say
"Women are from Venus, men are from Mars"
Enlightening the difference between women and men

"*Nyamasase*" is Venus

The first evening star and Morningstar
Faithful like a woman, indeed
Whose heart has not been rotten by a man
Named after a Roman queen
A true beauty full of love

I stand for Venus
Whose brightness competes with that of the moon
Which orbits the sun clockwise in retrograde rotation
While the other planets orbit anticlockwise on their axes
The hottest planet in the Solar System

I illuminate the issue of gender equality
With the brightness of Venus
Let's move with the time like Venus
Let's change our consciousness
In the love and beauty of Venus

Men and women are indeed different
Only in thought and how we were made
This does not mean our rights should be different
We were all created in the image of God
In His eyes, we are not different

In the original gender equality poem "Nyamasase", the poet uses the characteristics of the planet Venus to employ the "women are from Venus, men are from Mars" concept, to reveal that although men and women think differently or are biologically different, they should not be treated differently.

Cakes with no icing

There are women who put each other down
They criticise other women's presentation
And declare other women ugly
Simply because they do not straighten their hair
Or braid their hair
Or wear wigs
There are women labelled too fat
Or too thin
Then those who choose to not shave
Their armpits, private bits, legs and chins
There are some who do not shape their eyebrows
Or decorate their faces and nails

These women have those who appreciate them
It is quite common to find them taken
While the beauty queens remain untouched

Why is this the case, I wonder?

What do these women hinge on?
They must be delicious, these women
I say they are cakes with no icing

May I ask the beauty and slay queens
And those obsessed with how they look
You may carry on, but I'll make a small point
Too much sugar will trigger illness
Not everyone is looking for icing
Not everyone is into sugar
You may dismiss mbodza, but is it not filling?

Every guineafowl wears attractive spotted feathers
Do not criticise!
Cakes with no icing

The original poem "Makeke asina kirimu" encourages women to stop putting each other down.

Elderly white man

The love of my life
The one who owned my heart
Got tired of it and ravaged it
Then he found *one who only bathes on Saturday*
Each time he stepped out on a Saturday
He was busy philandering in guesthouses
Till out of the blue I caught from him an infection
Then realised the time was right to emigrate
My heart was ragged inside my chest
My mind wandered as I clenched my jaw

Brrrriiiing brrrriiiiing! My mobile phone rings
If it isn't my dear friend who now lives overseas!
She gets hold of me and entices me to join her
"Do not succumb to heartbreak by *drum piercers*
These town boys who don't date to marry
I have my elderly gentleman who actually married me
He has a friend looking for a woman to marry"
I pack my bags to go and see for myself
If it doesn't work out I'll grind like everyone else

I arrive in the land of cold and find him awaiting
My elderly white man, who looks just like *Mutemeregwa*
The headman of my mother's village in *Mberengwa*
More delicious to me than *mutetenegwa*
He likes me so much he could give me a piggyback
And loves me to the point of wanting to preserve me
All is well for me, I am still loveable
Age is just a number, it is not a big deal
He gently patches up my broken heart
He surprisingly has quite a good heart
We are used to the callous white Africans
The *kneeless ones* who colonised our country
Who with a simple gaze caused you to freeze

I am full of joy now in the land of whites
Where I spend all day speaking in English
Cooking for my man until his stomach is inflated
My heart is clear and holds no grudges
I am now contemplating having a baby
To strengthen the relationship with my elderly white man

In the original poem "Dhara rechirungu" the poet takes the persona of a young Zimbabwean woman who falls in love with an elderly white gentleman after losing hope in love following a painful heartbreak, thereby advocating human diversity.

Beautiful just the way you are

You are beautiful just the way you are
Love yourself as you are, girl child
Please be proud of who you are
That which is good must be taken as is
Milk is taken without salt
Do not accept *deflation by insects*
That feel elevated by bringing others down
Real beauty is found in your heart
Not in the clothes you wear
Not in the wigs you put on
Not in the hair stuck on your head
Not in the paint on your face
A cake with no icing is still delicious
It is commendable to beautify yourself
But this is pointless if your heart is not clean
Addiction to artificial beauty is pointless
Because most of you will know this
Beautiful calabashes sour the beer

A fair woman is either a witch or a thief
Not all well-garnished food is delicious
Before you transform externally
Consider looking within first
If you are a fight inciter
Employing blood sport for entertainment
Fix your deeds, not your face
If you are a homewrecker
Do unto others as you would have them do unto you
If you are a thief, floozy or loafer
Fix your deeds first, not your face
A crow remains black regardless of how much it washes
Altering yourself is an insult to your creator
A kraal worm living in dung thinks it is a cow too
If you were born dark skinned
Your skin tone is not a crime
Condemning the craftsmanship of your creator is
If you were born an albino
You are beautiful just the way you are

It is impossible for pregnancy to be aborted by coughing
You are who you are
If you denounce it, there's nothing to be done
And if you self-loathe, think about this
You have a deep-seated issue
Of not loving yourself as you are
Even if you transform your external self
The issue inside you will not disappear
An elephant is not burdened by its own tusks
If you believe you are not beautiful
If you feel ashamed of who you are
Those are your God-given tusks
Carry your tusks with pride like an elephant
Understand your life purpose, that is the beauty in you
Know where you're from and understand your journey
The place of birth is the place of life blessings

The original poem "Makanaka makadero" empowers women to love and accept themselves as they are.

Letter to the girl child

Misiinosiyana, girl child
You are in the here and now, pay attention
Sharpen your ears well, hear what I have to say
You are an extension of no one, you are not an offshoot
Believe in yourself, and everything you do
You are precious, you are a gem
You are beautiful just the way you are
You are not a toy, do not allow time wasters to use you
You are brave, trustworthy, loving and lovable
Where there is trust and love, there is no envy
Be proud of who you are, you are loved as you are
Do not allow narcissists to put you down
Do not compare yourself to others, we are all different
Yesterday will not remain yesterday, no two days are the same
You have a pure heart, be proud of your kindness
Even when others are being mean to you
You are bright girl child, but sometimes you will be challenged
Forgive yourself whenever you get it wrong
Ask for forgiveness from the bottom of your heart
You will find that others will forgive you too
In your failures, great lessons are learnt
Asking for help does not denote failure
Whatever you put your mind to is achievable
Accept what you cannot change
Your voice is precious, use it girl child
Ask and it shall be given
Laugh often and live a life of joy
But you are not a floozy, you are a counselled child
When sadness comes, accept it, it will pass
Consume what builds your body, and limit junk food
Exercise your body and you will live longer
Relax and find time for leisure to reduce sadness
Respect your body, it is the temple of God
Do not allow time wasters to play on it
Work hard, seek and you will find
Play hard, knock and you will receive
Respect others, and they will respect you too
Even during times of disagreement
Be mindful of the words that come out of your mouth
Encourage peace to thrive in your head

So that your mind remains at ease
Drive out rotten thoughts from your head
Pay attention to what your parents teach you
Do not deliberately distress your parents
But do tell them what's in your heart and mind
You will find they do good for you always
One day your parents will perish
But remember, you have a Father in heaven
Love and trust in Him, God our creator

The original poem "Mwadhi kumwanasikana" provides positive affirmations that every girl child should be equipped with, in order to know her self-worth and to keep her grounded. The letter is addressed to Misiinosiyana the poet's daughter, but it applies to all daughters of the world, of all ages and backgrounds.

Craving for "mutakura"

By its own choice, the tortoise has a shell
When the craving for *mutakura* attacks
Nothing else gives, nothing else matters
Until the right inoculation is administered
I prefer the one with maize and peanuts
If I graze that for breakfast
My lethargy and dizziness grinds to a halt

I woke up with the craving today
I must cook *mutakura* in my clay pot today
I overturned all baskets and found nothing
Maize kernels, peanuts, not a single grain
Oh dear, what do I do? I will not make it today
On the phone to friends and family I'm searching
The outlook is grim, and I turn to the internet
I have Googled and Googled, it looks promising
Finally, I find some maize on eBay
But the maize is sold as fish bait
I find some peanuts on Amazon
But the peanuts are sold as food for birds
What do I do………………………………….?
The craving is ravaging I will have to settle
My ingredients arrive the very next day
And I find that truly, it is food meant for animals
The grains are dirty and not meant for humans
My craving inner voice whispers, "that ain't a big deal
Select the good grains and have your feast
If you clean it up, you'll find it's not a massive task"
As I clean the grains, I reminisce my childhood
When I shelled maize cobs with *Mbuya*
And winnowed the grains before sending them to mill
I complete the task and place my pot on fire
Momentarily the aroma gusts into my space… it's ready!
As I gormandise *mutakura*, my heart is filled with joy
The burden of one's choice is never felt

The original poem "Havi yomutakura" directly translates to "craving for mutakura" is humorously delivered to describe a craving for mutakura and how the internet saves the day.

Flame Lily

The land of Zimbabwe
Selected a national flower
The beautiful Flame Lily
Even Queen Eliza
Has a Flame Lily brooch
A gift she was given
When she visited Zimbabwe

Colours of the Flame Lily
Remind me of the flag of Zimbabwe
Its shade of red
Reminds me of the bloodshed
Its yellow tone
Reminds me of the wealth and minerals
Its green pigment
Reminds me of the vegetation and agriculture
It sometimes has a tinge of white
Which makes me yearn for peace

There is no other flower
Suitable for Zimbabwe
Than the Flame Lily
I feel free, but yearn for liberty
As I gaze at the Flame Lily
As beautiful as the Great Zimbabwe
Oh, the Flame Lily!

The original poem "Nyakajongwe" is a praise poem for the Flame Lily plant, the official national flower of Zimbabwe. This poem highlights the beauty of the Flame Lily, with colours matching those on the Zimbabwean national flag.

Loves and likes

Social media wreaks havoc on humanity
Some do not rest, day and night
Some struggle to fall asleep
In pursuit of loves and likes
I mean being worshipped and adored
If it weren't for loves and likes
We would not be seeing absurdity
When we lounge on social media

Who are these hunters,
Of loves and likes
Who live to please the masses?

They get involved in whatever's happening
And spread and share whatever's happening
As and when it is occuring, livening
In order to please the world, tokening
In return for loves and likes, burdening!

It ends there on social media
On a day of misfortune, you will not find them
It is just a lounging place to inflate egos
It is what it is, just loves and likes

The original poem "Maravhu nemaraiki" is about "loves" and "likes" on social media and the sham of the charade.

Friend

I thought you were a friend close to my heart
And I shared with you the problems of my heart
        The ones regarding the pain of my heart
            You laughed so hard you could have cracked your heart
                Gosh you honestly have a hardened heart
                    Your behaviour rotted my heart
                I learnt what was in your heart
           That you cared not for my broken heart
        I now focus on healing my heart
    But you still are a friend close to my heart

The original poem "Sahwira" is about a disgruntled friend let down by a mate she thought was very close, whom she still loves dearly.

Over the contour ridge

All the dirt and fruit peels
Everything vile and disgusting
Everything that puts us to the test
Everything that spoils the yard
Must be chucked over the contour ridge

All those who cross our boundaries
And those who judge and weigh us on scales
Those who turn antisocial when drunk
Those used to being whipped to get back on track
And those with behaviours that prick like cactus spines
Those with self-inflicted problems that fill up a cart
Those with burdens heavier than a plough
Who choose to irritate others like pork fat
Just so they can reduce what troubles their souls
They will never make us cough, oho!
We are in order like a nice set of buns

We do not have energy to waste on it
We do not have time to be made sick by polony
What goes around comes around, karma will sort them
The way I see it, it is better this way
Let's chuck it all far, over the contour ridge

The original poem "Seri kwegandiwa" carries encouragement to unapologetically discard toxic relationships, interactions and behaviours, in order to enrich ourselves and live happier lives. In the rural areas of Zimbabwe, organic matter is habitually discarded over the contour ridge to help enrich the soil for crop farming.

Dolls and melons

I enter my bachelor friend's home starving
He volunteered to babysit while I worked all day!
"What's in your fridge today?
Oh, there's a melon, can't wait to tuck in!"
My hand is grabbed with force
"You can't have this one, it's my wife
Who I will warm up tonight when I'm on my own
Don't judge me, girlfriend, I have no ego
I gave up on real women a long time ago"

While using his bathroom before I leave
An object in his shower grabs my attention
Behind the curtain, a woman bends over
I unveil the curtain to find a mannequin
It has naughty bits! This is too much for me!
"Dear friend what is it I am seeing here?"
"Oh, that's just my other wife, don't judge me
My polygamous life is peaceful and joyous
When I want to have fun, I have no problems
The loves of my life are dolls and melons!"

I enter my car and make my way home
And ruminate on the multitude of spinsters I know
Who claim to be exhausted by heartbreak
By time wasting men of today who are *drum piercers*
And yet bachelors also claim they are exhausted
By spinsters who are too worldly and independent
Who talk too much, even *flies can't land on their lips*
They want to rule the home, they say
What on earth causes this social quandary?

Pursuing a squirrel's milk, instead of cow's milk!
Oh, I give up, what do I know?
On arrival at home I find Soko bought me a melon
Which I devour whilst admiring my children
As they play with dolls and also eat melon!

The original poem "Zvidhori namavise" highlights how people who have given up on relationships (possibly due to the prevalent issue of identity crisis amongst immigrants, as well as misaligned values and failure to integrate and diversify) are resorting to mannequins and vegetables to meet sexual needs.

Willow tree

Try new things and be open to change
Be malleable like a willow tree
Which can be braided and folded without breaking
If you know who you are you will not break
When you try new ways of doing things
And learning a variety of things
And being different things
Just like a willow tree

The old order changes yielding place to new
Things that do not end are an illusion
Today we may be happy
Tomorrow we may be sad
But if you're malleable like a willow
You positively embrace such changes
But do not be easily influenced like a fool
You will not be underrated for being reserved

Know when to argue
Know when to stop eating
Know when to stop drinking
Know when to open your mouth
Know the laws of where you are
Know who and what to trust

Be flexible and open
But also, strong and principled
Know where you come from
And where you're going
Like a train that wriggles
But remains on the rail track
You will be in receipt of varying rewards
And will be exposed to various opportunities
And you will be built just like a willow tree

In the original poem "Mufokosiyana", the poet encourages her readers to be malleable like a willow tree. In spirituality, using your freewill to be flexible enough to surrender to the universe presents more opportunities in life than when you are resistant.

Acquired through sweat

I grew up to the disturbing noise
Of the envious who labelled me child of a lord
Clearly, they had no idea
The lord raised an independent entity
Who taught me *the only thing for free is sunlight*
Everything else in life is worked for
In *Masvingo*, we bought bread from *Cheziya* bakery
As an adult, I work to acquire everything through sweat
I am however still subjected to noise
By those who reckon all I have
Was luck that came on a golden teaspoon

Sharpen your ears and hear me now
I work hard in all I do
I have *eaten many Bs*
That's not easy, do you want to bet?
Try it and you'll experience the magic
That happens when you cross the bridge
I have many jobs and a great purpose in life
I am a mother, wife, farmer
Seamstress, cook, therapist
I braid hair and knit
I am a lawyer, a poet, a writer, a teacher
I do a lot; I couldn't possibly list it all
There is nothing I don't cook
Sadza, mutakura, as well as baking cakes
I could also roast you some *mutetenegwa*
To many people, I'm an agony aunt
In my home, I am the maid, without hesitation
I'm also a modern but humble woman
To my husband, I remain competent
That is why I am loved deeply

Daily, I don't stop learning
I am never too lazy to teach others
The thirst for knowledge in me
Is not quenched easily, I have a long way to go
When the wise speak
My ears, like a rabbit's ears are open
If you have ears, you too should open them
When I grab my phone, I'm usually in search of knowledge
Never to look for being loved and liked
An ego massage from those who care not for me
I mean social media loves and likes
Knowing and loving God beats everything
Remember he sees all you think and do
Taking care of yourself is the centre pole
That makes all you do possible
I don't binge on alcohol
I consume food mindfully
I don't take shortcuts, one step at a time
The journey is long, you can't afford to be wobbly
I don't have time to measure other people's progress
I care not about what others think
I care not for worldly things
I have very limited time here on earth
My spirit has a long way to go
Flesh from the dust will return to dust
Because of this, I fear not my death

I do not have hesitant body parts
I am not afraid of sweat
I work hard
There's no luck
Please applaud me
I do not hesitate to sweat
I eat only what's acquired through sweat

In the original poem "Cheziya" the poet unapologetically challenges the assumption that those born into privileged families do not have to work hard for anything.

Sleep paralysis

Soko is working away again
My heart is restless
Due to the arduous task ahead
When it returns to haunt me tonight
I am ever so grateful, uncle Benjy
For the rosary from Medjugorje
The holy land you visited the other year
A crucifix now hung in my chamber of sleep
Mother Mary looks after me, nothing can touch me
All corners of my home are covered in salt
As the incense burns, I breathe holy scents
Dark spirit be gone, you can't touch me
I burn white sage to clear bad auras
I want not darkness, so I say a prayer
I gather my crystal gems, their energies protect me
If I place them where I lay my heavy head
Which from day to day will not stop throbbing
I devour several sedatives
Then slip into a hot bath
Saturated by Himalayan pink salt
Delightful Magnesium and Epsom salts
And a few drops of French lavender oil
The bathroom is ablaze
With several scented candles
Full of fragrant oils to calm my mind
A beautiful aroma wraps around me like a child
I feel like I'm in heaven
Relaxed in my bath
I feel at peace as I prepare for sleep
By the time it comes I'll be fast asleep
I keep the lights on, they're known to deter it
I put out just the candles as I prepare for sleep
Soon after my bath… A POWER CUT!
Why do we live in the sticks where power cuts occur?
Darkness stares at me, it's ready to play
My heart is pounding, my chest will explode
Dear God, what do you want me to do?
I tip toe slowly headed to my children's bedroom
"Come and sleep with me as your father's away"
"No thanks mummy, we were already asleep"

Oh dear…
I drag my feet headed for war
Which I can neither escape nor win
I peel off my clothing and get into bed
Sleep where are you, I've been waiting for a while?

Alas, I can sense a thing next to me
An attempt to scan it reveals the Three Days of Darkness
Could this be a so-called apparition?
Guardian angels, my ancestors, please protect me
Where are you those of my clan?
My breath ceases as my heart pounds on

For pity's sake, it better not be an incubus!
If it is then bugger off, my yoni is divine!
Is it you Diablo brandishing your trident?
I lie static as my energy depletes
What do I do? All I want is peace!
I feel so hot even my head is baking
Hidden under my quilt on a hot summer night

Sweat trickles down my face like a gentle brook
A euphonious throb, as blood pumps through my veins
Makes me conscious of an inevitable war, as I hug myself tight

Dark spirit you're back, greetings to you!
"Get up, let's play!" it kindly responds
"Apologies honey, I'm a bit late tonight"
Then it climbs onto me like an equestrian
As I attempt to escape, my muscles decline
My open orifice, fails to release a scream
When sleep paralysis comes, *calls become inaudible*
It electrifies me with its heavy pressing
It rides me proper and warns me, "Watch your back!"
Like a stallion, it prances on me as if a bet was placed on it
It's an all-nighter it's going nowhere
Feels like torrential rain, Lord have mercy!
I fight it, I writhe, its thirst remains unquenched!

I call upon our Father in heaven
"Father, an adversity truly befalls me
Please be with me during this very difficult time
Please pluck this thing off me

And chuck it far enough to flow away with the river
God if you're taking me please forgive my sins
I have so many sins, I'm so sorry I'm a sinner
God, Father please look after my family when I'm gone
Lord Father…"
It stops. It's gone. Shhhhhh

Snoring takes over as my heart begins to rest
I escape to dreamland as my mind unwinds
A few fleeting winks later…beep! beep! beep! beep!
My mobile phone alarm sounds
The sun is out, hooray! hooray!
I made it! I'm alive!
With bloodshot eyes, I'm grateful for grace
"Dark spirit, have a great day
See you soon, when you return".

The original rhyming poem "Dzikirira" describes a horrific sleep paralysis incident.

Machonyonyo

They spot each other in the bar, it's happening tonight
Voluptuous woman with a troubled mind is partying
She wears a "*musandizeza*", he won't let her escape
The bouncer wearing tight clothes muses
"Check me out, I'm hefty, and have veins in my arms
I have a massive meaty six pack"
His eyes are traps to all, he doesn't hesitate
The bar is dark like the Three Days of Darkness
But his piercing gaze is deep and razor-sharp
They guzzle cocktails and champagne
Like maize beverage at a work-for-beer party in Africa
"*Alcohol makes old wives wenches*", the Zezuru were right
The sybaritic target bends and writhes like a python
Her micro-frock rides up like a flag being raised
Her corpulent bits stray, like lard flowing out of a covered pot
Sweat streams uncontrollably, offering an inescapable stench
The music blasting is Zim dancehall
Provocative dancing, makes them *deaf to calls*
Grinning mischievously like a Cheshire cat
He imagines pulling, her accepting…he's in!
They exit the bar and enter a car

When the deed is done they waltz in dreamland
The sun has risen, and the bar is shut
The police tap the window and shout "wake up!"
Calls are now inaudible, amidst the loud snoring
They dream of being back home
In rural *Chivi*, they call it *Machonyonyo*
But they will end up incarcerated
Due to losing their morals in public
These *machonyonyo* acting like little children

The original poem "Machonyonyo" translates to "promiscuous people", a derogatory term used by the Karanga. "Machonyonyo" is also a Karanga word used to describe very remote rural areas in Zimbabwe. The poet plays with the two meanings to describe a one-night stand.

That which pleases daddy

i enter
    the quilt,
        he's asleep.
           he turns,
              looks at me.

his arm
    is on,
        my belly button
           he strokes it,
going south,
    it tickles.
        he massages
           my
              bottom
                  pooch.
he breathes
    to the warmth
      of my
        booty
           i turn.
              he smiles.
in his sleep.
    i'm happy.
        he's pleased with,
           that which pleases daddy.

The original poem "Chifadzababa" describes a husband/lover's appreciation of their wife/partner's belly pooch. The poem encourages women to be proud of their bodies.

Condolences from the bewitcher

IF I did you wrong, I'm sorry
NOT SURE why. It's a generational spiritual problem
I may be *possessed by a spirit of an ancestor*
Please forgive me
I am a man of flesh
I have NO IDEA what possessed me
I will not do it again
Forgive me, my friend
The spirits took the best of me
I DON'T KNOW how they manage to possess me
I will not repeat it
See how much I have lamented
Do you want me to kneel?

Be enough! Like bus fare should be, child of my country!
You have taken no responsibility for your wrongs!
If your spirits have caused everything
And you have no idea how they possessed you
How do you know you'll not repeat the offence?
Hit the highway, man of flesh!
You and your spirits, have a safe trip
Even I am possessed and am a man of flesh

The original poem "Kubaqhwa mavoko nanyakuroya" reprimands inauthentic apologies from people who find it difficult to take responsibility for their actions.

Money back home

It is good to send money back home
So that they may drink all day
Using money you earned washing the elderly

It is good to build a mansion back home
Where you do not know when you will return
Yet you live on an empty purse

It is good to have a house built on your behalf
Where you send money month after month
When you check progress, you find bare ground

It is good to send money back home
So they can eat eggs and boerewors
While you live on unbuttered bread

It is good to send money back home
So they can go on holiday
Yet for many years you have not taken a break

It is good to send money back home
To the thankless ones, you know who they are
They return tomorrow saying what you give is not enough

It is good to send money back home
So you can hear them saying they miss and love you so
Yet upon receipt of funds, you hear nothing more

It is good to send money back home
To those who get worked up when you say you have nothing
Yet they don't think of you when they get it elsewhere

It is good to send money back home
All their conversations with you are about money
They want nothing else from you

It is good to send money back home
But ask yourself, what if you die tomorrow?
Be contented, be mindful, before you send money back home

The original poem "Mari kumusha" highlights the importance of being mindful when sending funds from the diaspora to relatives and friends back home.

Vandal

In a ghetto location
He took her
Before she was ripe
And gave her the bottle
Then vandalised her
Who could she tell?

Through the grapevine she heard
He vandalised again
Then was reported
And he served in prison
The vandal himself.

At a station in London
Whilst waiting for a train
At the crack of dawn
She saw a man
Standing with a girl
Who was not yet ripe
She scrutinised him
And it was him!
The vandal himself.

She charged towards him
All her energy amassed
Straight from the core
Then propelled to his face
A gift on the nutcracker!

The original poem "Muchinyiri" describes a situation where an underaged girl is raped back in Zimbabwe but is unable to speak up at the time the crime takes place. Many years later, whilst waiting for a train at a London railway station, the victim spots a man in the company of an underaged girl, identifies him as her rapist (perchance a delusion) and punches him in the face.

May I have it, I want it

The year commences, we arrive at boarding school
As I furtively grab fried chicken from my trunk
And take a little comforting bite
A hand arrives, "may I have some?"
Days go by and I miss *mutetenegwa*
That I hid behind my clothes at the top of my wardrobe
I open, scoop a few, covertly chew and the aroma travels
A hand arrives, "may I have some?"
Weeks go by and I miss tinned beef
I discreetly attempt to open it, the lid breaks, how unfortunate!
A hand arrives, "let me open that for you!"
Soon as it opens, I hear "may I have some?"

We grow up, work and are living life
Brother buys a car, "I want it!"
Sister finds a husband, "I want him!"
Successful friend is doing well, "I want it!"
Others work hard and make it in life, "I want it!"
Relative buys a mansion, "I want it!"
All of it "I said I want it!"

What a struggle you harbour in your head
Lover of things …
You say you want everything
Have you ever wondered whether you love yourself?

In the original poem "Ndipevo, ndozvidavo" the poet captures behaviour of people who are always after other people's things and are never satisfied with their own. They are usually barely innovative and feel extremely entitled. She wonders if this is somewhat linked to their lack of self-love, a void which only they can fill.

I don't know you

You and I are close
But you seem to have an enigmatic plight
You seem to be plagued with envy
Seems to surface when you've had a drink
Your attitude makes my head spin
Like the herbs you like to smoke
You act normal by day
And act like you can love
Then by night a complete transformation
Into a coward who won't address their issues
Can never fall asleep without binging on it first
You lose your mindfulness and begin the nonsense
Talking too much, rowdiness, flirting
You seem to be *possessed by some ancestral spirit*
Especially when you're cheered on
You have no problem with shaking for an audience
Nor pulling the married ones while you're at it
Your intention being to hurt
You respect no one
When the spirits possess you
There is evil intended
There is jealousy in it
There is childishness in it
You have no love inside you
You are rotten inside
What will my kids learn from you?
What you say is not aligned with what you do
I tried to counsel and help you
But you said you do as you please
Ego is your biggest issue
You're a prisoner of worldly things
You're great at making people believe your lies
You confuse me like a two-headed snake
Do as you please, but you cannot get near me
There is a thistle hedge you cannot hurdle
That I planted to protect myself from your gaslighting
I can see you need love, but you're not lovable
It seems you hurt because you are hurt
From the problems you carry
That seem terminal

That you won't acknowledge
You do not listen, or grow up
It's arduous to respect, or trust you
I don't know you

In the original poem, "Handikuzivi" translates to "I don't know you."

In the Lord's name

They did well the Dutch Reformed Church who taught her
"In the name of the Lord is where I reside"
Now they are here, trials and tribulations
She cries and calls out His name
The Lord's name is where she lives!

Hit by a cold snap she misses home
She stands by the window in contemplation
A quiet voice comes and whispers to her
Look to your right, do you see that stream
Look to your left, do you see trees and flowers
Do not cry, God is with you, do you not see?
The greatest thing is love; you will see!

She pursues her career
A learned female *child of my aunt*
She annoys the unconscious incompetents
Until they dismiss her from work
She cries out loud and the whisper returns
Plough on girl child, God is with you

Her home heats up, there are too many bulls in it
Husband is a bull, wife is a bull, children are bulls
What can they do, that is the life here in the West?
Never mind, bulls are an illusion
We are definitely all one being
We all came from the Source
With this enlightenment, her heart is freed!

They did well the Dutch Reformed Church who taught her
"In the name of the Lord is where I reside"
Now they're gone, her trials and tribulations
She laughs out loud and calls out His name
The Lord's name is where she lives!

In the original poem "Muzita rashe" the poet expresses that her faith sees her through trials and tribulations, time and time again.

You've gone Madhuve

You've gone *Madhuve*!
You've gone *Madhuve*, to the ungrateful maKaranga
You've gone *Madhuve*, leaving rain in *Harare*
Leaving abundance for famine in *Chivi*
You've gone *Madhuve*, you're now married
Congratulations your maturity has made us proud
Congratulations you've had four healthy kids
VaKaranga be grateful, see *Madhuve* has done well

Get over yourselves maZezuru, you're not learned
Get over yourselves, our son is good-looking
We have no idea why he settled for this
We settled the dowry payment *Mazvimbakupa*
Besides she was dirt cheap, so we'll treat her like dirt
We're tired of her, *she has become watery*
Plus, she's a witch who brings us shame

You've gone *Madhuve*, to the land of *kneeless ones*
You've sought refuge from the troubling maKaranga
You've gone *Madhuve*, to be a nurse in a cold overseas country
You've gone *Madhuve*, with your children
You've escaped *Madhuve*, unable to deal with the maKaranga
There she has gone!

After a while, *Madhuve* falls ill
Cancer of the cervix, oh dear, poor soul
The tumours were malignant, and it was too late
She fought a good fight then *Madhuve* bade farewell
You've gone *Madhuve*, and left the problems of this world
You've gone *Madhuve*, to an unreachable heaven
You've gone *Madhuve*, rest in peace

In the original poem "Wainda Madhuve" the poet describes how an unappreciated good wife is rejected, mistreated and emotionally abused by her in-laws, then decides to emigrate to the UK, where she eventually suffers from cancer and dies. "Madhuve" is a praise name for females of the Zebra totem.

I have dug a little hole

Exhausted by darkness
I give in to the burden of life
I struggle to harvest after planting and cultivating
I have waited for rain to grow the fruit of my toil
I have made an effort, I really have
And now *I dig a little hole*, I refuse this

God, I'm ready to come to you
"Stay there my child, your time will come"
Mother, please intercede the time is now
"Stay there my child and look after your children"
Grandma look there is no joy here
"Stay there my grandchild, joy will come"
Dear aunt, please visit my dreams
Dear uncle, please visit my dreams
You ended your lives, what's it like where you are?
"Stay put dear child, killing yourself solves nothing
You are there to learn life lessons
If you escape before your time
God will reincarnate you undoubtedly
Your time will come when you have learnt"
I have dug a little hole, I want to learn

Then enlightenment comes to me
Then joy manifests in me
Then strength and willpower live in me
In this world, I want to gain knowledge
In this world, I want to share my knowledge
I now know my purpose in life

My spirit can rest now
I have dug a little hole

The original poem "Chikomba ndachera" describes the feeling of being exhausted by depression, thoughts of suicide and then enlightenment. Digging a little hole is a symbolic act performed in Zimbabwe to show that a lesson has been learnt. This is less common now, but children, after receiving corporal punishment, were instructed to dig a little hole and spit into it, a ritual to evidence commitment to never repeat the same misdemeanour.

Premature baby

I had always known
That when I gave birth
I would not be sure he'd live
With no love in the home
I was not sure I'd live
But with the baby I carried, I lived

Without it
I would not be here

Out of nowhere my uterus tore
I had got huge like a heifer

Come, my sweetheart
To ameliorate my aching heart

With only a month to go
You're here premature baby
We thought you wouldn't last a month
But today you're as big as the moon
I'm proud of you my star
My premature baby

The original poem "Gavamwedzi" is about a pregnant woman whose labour is triggered early due to a loveless relationship and stress associated with it; and how she welcomes the child as the one who will ease her pain.

Acting

Snap! Snap! Snap!
Pictures were taken
People were acting and acting

One year a man from back home
Visited his wife abroad
But due to his *miscellaneous behaviour*
The man dissected his mobile phone
Battery placed in his coat pocket
Sim card thrown in his trouser pocket
Memory card hidden in his bag
Other parts elsewhere

One day as the wife was tidying up
She found parts of the mobile phone
And knew something was amiss
She took the memory card to her night shift
Upon arrival she put it in her own phone
But found it locked with a PIN number
All night she thought of a plan
By sunrise she had devised an idea

Early morning when her shift ended
The woman headed to a photo shop
Got the memory card and asked, "please develop these"
She returned to the photoshop after a short while
Then was handed a pack of photographs
The *kneeless one* who passed the photos blushed
The woman found a bench in the town centre, and sat
Then opened the photo wallet to go through

Oh, looks like baby daddy is being sucked!
Dang, those are his feet and I know his knees!
OMG, they are in a hotel where he's taken me before!
Oh yes, I recognise the curtains, I know them too well!
Jees, looks like a mish mash of whores!
Oh, each photograph has a different whore!
Oh dear, some have flat boobs; some have tooth gaps!
Wow, some are light and some dark skinned!
Ow, the middle-aged woman gagged, then

Beuuuuuoooooooooooooooooooork
She vomited in the town centre!

After a while the woman found strength
Then returned home with the photographs
"What is this, father of my children?
Is this what you get up to in my absence back home?
Honestly look at how hard I work
All the money I send you ...
Spending it on whores, wrenching my heart like this?"

The man responded
"Mother of my children, your mind needs to be looked at
Your mind is lost, *children have been playing with it*
No one in their right mind does what you have done
This is absolutely unbelievable!
When I dissect my mobile phone
I do that out of respect for you
But you have clearly failed to respect me
Are you really still ok upstairs?"

The woman did not live for much longer
She died of a broken heart.
The man cried the loudest at the funeral

Snap! Snap! Snap!
Pictures were taken
Whilst the mischievous man
Was acting and acting

The original poem "KuEkita" encapsulates people who live lives full of drama, acting all the way, to the extent that they do not know who they are. The poem describes a cheating narcissistic husband based in Zimbabwe who confidently denies any wrongdoing and gaslights his wife who works in the diaspora and blames her for being the insane wrongdoer.

Player of the game

Life is a game
You are a player
To win the game
Sharpen your proficiency
Strengthen your body
Focus on healthy consumption
Sharpen your mind
Quiet your mind
Let go of your ego
Be loving
Help those who struggle
Do good
Even when no one's watching
With this you'll be the player
Of a big game
The game of life.

The original poem "Mutambi wemutambo" presents life as a game and gives tips on how to be a shrewd player at it.

Boundary crossing

Hey man, stop boundary crossing!
Stop disturbing the peace of others
See everyone plants a thistle for you
How I wish I could manhandle you
And *gift you one on the nutcracker*. Oops!
You're in luck, because
I fear God's judgement

Every time you overstep the line
I secretly wish for you to trip and fall
Got me wishing you had leprosy. Oops!
Then I remember God knows my thoughts
See, your disease spreads to rot us all
Your boundary crossing is rather contagious
Hey man, stop boundary crossing!

The original poem "Chifinhu" is slang for "boundary crossing" expresses frustration towards a habitual line stepper or boundary crosser, who causes the poet to inadvertently cross her lines of spiritual principles.

Springhare sort of sociopath

Since you have decided to deputise me as second wife
The audacity to replace me before my death
Sit down over there, let me spell it out in Karanga
These old traditions are old and dead to me
Are you not ashamed of your incestuous behaviour?
Clearly a wild dog that needs to be tamed
Wake up and stop this self-sabotage!
You're a springhare sort of sociopath

You come to my house acting like you're the shit
Gliding around, butt stuck up like a cocktail ant
Bringing chaos in our lives like a female mole cricket
You feel yourself like a purple crested lourie
But you're an antisocial sociopath who *pisses in water wells*
Who on earth taught you to be a homewrecker?
Wake up little ma'am before you get used!
You deplete my energy like a bed bug that bites its carrier

So you have decided to replace me
Yesterday's child who just stepped out of her nappies
Be careful dear, you'll shoot yourself with a catapult
You'll invoke a *vengeful spirit* which can't be appeased
I am the queen in this home, you can't walk all over me
Respect my man, the head of our home is not an untrained bull
Open your eyes little girl, don't devalue yourself!
You're a springhare sort of sociopath

In the original poem, "Chimusvatusvatu chimukandakavava" refers to one with 'loose morals'. The term could not be translated, so the poet made up "Springhare sort of sociopath". A Springhare is a Southern African rodent (known in Zimbabwe as "chidhure") which resembles a baby kangaroo; it is adorable to look at but is an opportunistic nuisance which waits for farmers to sow their seeds and when the seeds are moist and ready to germinate, it eats them all. In this poem, a woman has voluntarily moved into her older sister's home to take over as wife and mother. The older sister is in the diaspora, separated from her husband and children who are back home. This is a common occurrence, where families are separated due to emigration complications, and one spouse leaves while the other stays home. The poet assumes the persona of the disgruntled wife who refuses to be replaced. In Shona culture, it is acceptable for a younger sister or niece to 'replace' an older sister or an aunt who has died, cannot have children or no longer wants to sleep with her husband. The younger relative is simply 'given' as a gift to the relevant man. Although the practice is less prevalent, the poet takes a militant feminist approach towards this custom, which she views as grooming young girls into commodities and objects of male desire. Unfortunately, due to economic hardship or otherwise, the practice is used as an excuse by some women to 'take' relatives' spouses, as an easy escape.

Strength of a mad man

Sat in a little consultation room
I find myself face to face with a mind healer
After explaining everything that got me there
Explaining where I've been and where I'm going
The white man looks at me with teary eyes
With the strength of a mad man, I cease to blink

"It is not your fault you did not choose this
You are bold and have made it this far, keep going
The dysfunctional family in which you were raised
Has not yet healed from post-colonial stress
Caused by my dysfunctional family, my ancestors
They are the ones who brought you here!"
With the strength of a mad man, I hold my breath

"Your madness and that of your relatives
Are a result of fights between people in need
Fights amongst a people robbed
Misunderstandings of people seeking a way out
Fights amongst people lacking liberty
Fights amongst people deprived of a home"
With the strength of a mad man, I begin to see

So what do I do to heal my mind?
"Your mind is healed by your understanding."
What do I do to heal the minds of others?
"Their minds have got nothing to do with you"
What do I do when they begin to provoke me?
"It's just drama, your role is to refuse to act in it"
With the strength of a mad man, I totally get it

The original poem "Simba rebenzi" highlights the benefit of seeking professional help if depressed or suffering from other mental health issues. Sometimes an explanation and understanding of your history and how it impacted your upbringing provides an understanding of who you are and why you react the way you do in various situations. Having this understanding may be the very thing that heals your mind.

We seem to…

We seem to know each other from a past existence
We seem to mystically speak the same language
We seem to feel and understand each other
We seem to tickle and make each other happy
We seem comfortable to be authentic around each other
We seem to never criticise or belittle each other
We seem to encourage and lift each other up
We seem to educate and mentor each other
We seem to energise and give each other strength
We seem to intuitively know what the other needs
We seem to dream and daydream of each other
We seem related and have a cosmic connection
We seem to nourish and satisfy each other
We seem to like and fancy each other
We seem to love and adore each other

The original poem "Tinoita se" describes the tense, magnetic feeling of making a harmonious soul connection with another human being who resonates with you, usually when least expected, usually due to synchronicity - a metaphysical phenomenon.

Question

I have a question!
If a married woman prays
And a mistress prays also
Both asking for exclusive love, from the same man
To God who loves equally
Whose prayer is answered?

The original poem "Mubvunzo" poses a philosophical question.

See you in heaven

Is God for us all?
Does God love Heathens?
Does God love Christians?
Does God love Traditional Spiritualists?
Does God love Hindus?
Does God love Muslims?
Does God love Buddhists?
Does God love Jews?
Does God love New Age Spiritualists?
Does God love Atheists?

See you in heaven!

The original poem "Tovonana kudenga" emphasizes that despite our religious beliefs, we are one and God loves us all.

Root establishment

At what point will you stop considering yourself an outsider?
How can you be happy with a fettered heart?
Due to the lack of liberty
You are a plant uprooted from its natural habitat
Remember, you are thick-skinned like a dung-fortified house

Wherever you reside now
Even if you expect to return home
Even if you're an asylum seeker
Time and tide wait for no man, you may die tomorrow
Prepare for your death consciously, it is the only way
To be mindful and content daily
The world belongs to one owner
God in heaven who created the universe
Borders in this world were created by humans
Who will all die and exit the world
Refuse to live like a prisoner wherever you are
Refuse to be treated unfairly wherever you are
Be free as if you're in your mother's house
Be joyous as if you're in your father's house
Because this world was created by your Father

Do as you would do back home, live in the here and now
Respect the laws and discard badness, or they'll deport you
And they do not hesitate to imprison
Do good in order to grow and become established
You may build a house or start your own business
You may speak, influence, coach others to enlighten them
Or go fishing, or whatever you enjoy doing for leisure
Be free child, time waits for no man
You were uprooted but it is time
For your roots to establish and begin to grow

The original poem "Kudzika midzi" explores further the analogy of displaced people to plants uprooted from their natural habitat. The poet encourages immigrants in the diaspora to live their lives fully in the here and now, to feel at home wherever they are, in order to become grounded again, and thus start growing.

Chitende

Today Chitende lands here with a bang!
A feisty female, sounds like a percussion
Tickles your fancy with her words of truth
Aggravates men, especially the cowards
With words that sting like the kiss of a ground bee
Cause she wastes no time on obscure allusions
To all abusers, she says march and go!
Those full of mischief, clean your deeds with a swab
Should be ashamed of pissing in public
Trouncing women and knocking out their teeth
Us women want intimacy, not hit and runs
Let's not bother playing hide and seek
Because of you, our hearts are in tatters
The universe will punish you with adversity
Such bad luck, you will contract scabies
There's nothing else to say if your behaviour's sloppy
You'll itch all over, including your testicles
Do not judge her, she doesn't give a monkey's
She has roots in *Mazvihwa*, be grateful for her
She gives better counsel than that of agony aunts
You heard what you heard, Chitende drops her mic!

The original poem is a rhyming finale in which the poet sums up her mission to dismantle inequality and abuse.

"Chitende" is a Shona word for calabash or gourd, which is used on percussion instruments in Africa as an amplifier. Mbira, Hosho and Marimba are Zimbabwean examples of such instruments. Ironically, percussion is a musical instrument that is sounded usually by being struck with a beater.

The poet was nicknamed "Chitende" by her paternal grandmother, for being an outspoken child. Her outspokenness in a society where women were conditioned to be submissive, was indispensable music to her feminist ears. Unfortunately, a lot of women who challenge the patriarchy are susceptible to misogyny, an unpleasant plight the poet has had to fight time and time again. Misogyny, as she learnt the hard way, is not simply the hatred of women; instead, it's about controlling and punishing women who challenge male dominance. It rewards women who reinforce the status quo and punishes those who don't.

A calabash or gourd is also a traditional multipurpose household item treasured in Africa. As an impenetrable item, its uses range from storage of clothing, food, drinking water and tea. In some African cultures, it was traditionally used as a symbol of wealth. In this poem, Chitende's impenetrable and resilient character amplifies the discontent of women brought by abuse, social conditioning and inequality.

Uprooted interview (translated from Shona)

Editor: What is poetry to you, and can you take me through your process of writing it?

Poet: Poetry is a product of deep consciousness which is different from talking or storytelling. A poem is a story in itself, written like a song but without the gluing words that lengthen a story. The ability to produce a meaningful story without gluing words is the poet's challenge. They have to come up with a few powerful words that leave the reader satisfied. Poetry, like prose, is a reflection of real life. It touches what happens to us at home, work, and within our society. As such, there will always be a poem out there that resonates with a reader or someone they know. I love to empower, raise awareness and consciousness, as well as highlight what I think is right or wrong. For example, a person might be a victim of hidden abuse without realising it, due to their static cultural upbringing or religious beliefs that encourage forgiveness of repeat offenders. Such beliefs cultivate hidden abuse, misogyny and narcissism, which could have devastating effects on a person's wellbeing. The intention of culture and religion is good, but people need to be aware that there is a limit to the benefit of these beliefs (which were created by people by the way) and we should recognise when such beliefs are being used to manipulate and abuse others. Writing poetry begins as a personal journey which I would equate to writing in a diary that no one has access to, so my thoughts are authentic and precious to me. What happens after I pour my thoughts into "my diary" is I garnish them with various poetic devices to make them palatable to others. Sometimes the poems just come out ripe and ready to go, with nothing to add or subtract from them.

Editor: So this is your debut title – what inspired you to write it?
Poet: For a very long time I quietly observed life unfolding and thought I would like to write about some of my experiences. I have learnt a lot from life, directly and through others, and I feel the time is right to share some life lessons. I am an introvert but to people with whom I am close and comfortable, I use a lot of humour in conversation, and they have always asked when I would begin to write. I had a barrier in my mind which made me think I could not handle writing for leisure. Then I learnt to meditate, a practice that brings me close to God and sharpens my creativity. Words just flow to me like downloads through meditation.

Editor: How long did it take you to write the original poems in this collection?

Poet: It took a few months to write them, and I continue to write every day. I selected seventy-five poems that I felt were suitable for this collection. When I started writing, I would sometimes meditate and produce up to twenty poems a day. I would go back to edit some of the poetry whilst producing more.

Editor: And what does the title "Zvadzugwa Musango" mean?

Poet: I am a collector of rare exotic plants, specifically cacti and succulents. One of the lessons I learnt from looking after these plants is that, plants uprooted from their natural habitat serve a purpose of adorning our homes, but us home keepers sometimes forget that the soil in our gardens is different from the soil where the plants came from. In order for exotic plants to survive, they need conditions they are acclimatised to in nature. For example, if I found an Aloe that was growing in sandy or gritty soil near a hill, when I plant it in a pot, the soil I use for it must be sandy and gritty so that it is tricked into thinking it is still in its natural habitat. If a plant got little water in its natural habitat, then I too give it little water. I see Zimbabweans and other immigrants living in the diaspora as plants uprooted from their natural habitat. As such, they should not forget where they are from by losing their authenticity, so that they stay rooted and grounded wherever they are.

Editor: The original poetry is written in the Karanga dialect. Could you please illuminate your reasons for that?

Poet: I am proudly of Karanga origin and love speaking in that dialect. It is my desire to see more books written in this dialect so that it does not go extinct. My view is that a lot of Zimbabweans are hugely influenced by foreign cultures and do not make enough effort to learn and preserve their own. While it is important to embrace diversity, we must not forget who we are.

Editor: The things you write about – did they actually happen or are they figments of your imagination? Can you give examples?

Poet: Yes, there are personal experiences in my poetry, some are other people's experiences that evoke emotion and the energy to write. Sometimes I just remember a Karanga word that I like, and I find a story or life lesson to attach to it, so that I may raise awareness of that word and prevent its extinction. "When will you return" is a lamentation of the disappearance of my brother who went to South Africa and never returned. "It slipped" is a poem mourning the loss of an unborn child. This happened to me and many other women close to me. "Cancer" is a poem describing the hurt caused by the affliction, which took my mother and other close family and friends. Poems such as "Misfortune", "Adversity", Elderly white man" are experiences of other people that I felt the need to write about. Poems such as "Bones", "Dare me" "Take this needle" all started with Karanga words I liked the sound of, and I found themes and lessons to attach to those words and turned them into poems.

Editor: Am I right in thinking that you are drawn to issues such as equality and abuse of women?

Poet: You are right. The subjects of inequality and abuse are very important to me, because I am a woman and I have a daughter who will one day become a woman. I attribute the issues we're having to deal with as grownups to individual upbringings. My wish is for all children to be raised mindful of love, equality and positivity, to hopefully eliminate issues such as abuse and inequality in adulthood. These issues may seem unimportant to some, but they certainly affect the mental wellbeing of women, some of whom are mothers with a huge responsibility to raise children. The cycle must be disrupted. Some women end up in mental health institutions, and some commit suicide, depending on the extent of abuse to which they are subjected. It truly disturbs me that a creation of God might have such an effect on another creation. My anger on these matters is demonstrated in poems such as "Man is a bedbug" and "Possessed by the spirit of Manyuchi" to name a few. The poems also raise awareness to those who do not fully understand abuse and its outcomes.

Editor: What else could be done to remedy the issue of abuse, other than how we raise our children, given that the problem is rife now in adults?

Poet: I think if women were more united, respected each other more and lifted each other up, we would have a better chance of winning this war. Currently, we compete against each other, belittle each other, fight over men, and things like that. How do we win the battle for equality if we are abusing and weakening one another? If we as women carry on this way, we are strengthening the patriarchy and the abusers,and are cultivating the 'divide and conquer' ideology by weakening ourselves. The way I see it, any woman who hurts another woman is on the patriarchy's side in the battle for equality. I touch on these issues in poems such as "Cakes with no icing", "Beautiful just the way you are", and "Letter to the girl child". In "Damn it!" I congregate all women and encourage them to fight in unity against equality.

Another way we could help ourselves is by refusing to crown undeserving men as kings. I say to women, if a man does not treat you right and you treat them like a king, this gets you nowhere. It is better to outright declare that you are precious and should be treated as such. The poems "My lord", "Jackal", "Blessed to be Vhudzijena's" and "Corona" address this point.

Poet: How did you as the editor find the poetry?

Editor: As the elders say, *eye-witnessing produces a fuller account of an event than hearsay.* I learnt a lot from this poetry, and I was thoroughly fascinated by it. In most of the poems, I know at least one person who the poem might relate to. I cannot wait for my own daughters to grow up to read and learn from this book.

Poet: Could you talk through three of your favourite poems from this collection and why they appeal to you?

Editor: Why would you choose to corner me like this? I feel like a parent who has been asked to name their favourite child. Anyway, I will attempt to answer your question. Let me start with "Jackal". This poem is weaved using several poetic devices that leave me riveted by how you were able to come up with the word combination. The poem is hilarious yet rhymes throughout, whilst thoroughly scrutinising the energy depleting behaviour of a foolish man. Then "Sleep paralysis", something I experience myself if I fall asleep on my back. The story told in this poem reminds me of sleep paralysis, how the experience terrifies me when it is happening, and how I laugh it off afterwards. Even the way the verses are arranged in the poem induce a minor sleep paralysis attack on me as I read the poem. Finally, "Mother's Tongue". The issue of our African languages is crucial. It is believed that if you want to destroy a people, you start by destroying their culture. Our culture is engraved in our language, so death of our languages is death of our culture, and we end up as people with no roots, *trailing blindly where we are persecuted like mice.* So this poem which encourages the preservation of our mothers' tongue warms the cockles of my heart.

Poet: I believe you are the first to write in Karanga, spelling out the onomatopoeic sounds of the dialect. When I read your novel "*Mazai eMheni*" I was motivated to follow suit and spell out the sounds of the Karanga dialect. What is your message to successive writers on this matter?

Editor: The first thing is, I was not the first to write in Karanga. If you look at the early Shona bibles, they were written in Karanga, using "X" for example to bring out the sound of the dialect. I however took this further and wrote the words as I heard them, in order to preserve how the dialect is actually spoken, by using alphabetical letters such as "Q" and "L". To the writers of today and tomorrow, I say be free to write as you speak. This is very important in the preservation of our good traditions. *A lizard suns itself within view of its hiding place.* I feel elated and am honoured that another author saw what I did, followed suit, and encouraged it.

******************** The end********************

Glossary of terms

Ara uru – Children's game
Baba – father
Chamuvande-vande – Children's game, hide and seek
Chando – Winter (season of the year) / cold
Cheziya – acquired through sweat / that of sweat
Chikumi – June
Chikunguru – July
China – Thursday
Chipikiri – Aphrodisiac; nail
Chipiri – Tuesday
Chirimo – Spring (season of the year)
Chishanu – Friday
Chitatu – Wednesday
Chisveru – Children's game, tag / you're it
Chivabvu – month of May
Dudu muduri – children's game
Ehuhuweeee – the opening line of a Shona lullaby
Gumi – ten
Gumi neimwe – eleven
Gumiguru – October
Gunyana – September
Igwe – a title of respect and honour in Igboland (Nigeria)
Ina – four
Kamani – Shona expression derived from the English phrase "come on"
Kubvumbi – April
Kukadzi – February
Kurume – March
Kutamburahuda – Poverty is a choice (name of a band)
Mai – mother
Matsutso – Late midsummer, when crops are about to ripen (season of the year)
Mbodza – undercooked sadza (thick maize porridge)
Mbudzi – November / goat
Mbuya – grandmother
Motsi – one
Muchemedzambuya – aphrodisiac from White Cheesewood tree
Mugondorosi – aphrodisiac from the Sausage tree
Mugovera – Saturday
Mujubheki – South African (the Shona word is derived from Jo'burg)
Musandizeza – don't hold back

Mutakura – a traditional Zimbabwean snack comprising boiled maize kernels and peanuts
Mutetenegwa – salted roasted peanuts
Muvhuro – Monday
Ndira – January
Nomwe – seven
Nyamasase – also known as Nyamatsatsi in other Shona dialects, is the planet Venus
Nyamavhuvhu – August
Ona – look; see
Pada – Children's game, hopscotch
Pfumbamwe – nine
Piri – two
Sadza – thick maize meal porridge (Zimbabwe's staple starch)
Sere – eight
Shanu – five
Shewe – a common hallowed title by which husbands of the older generation are addressed by their wives in Zimbabwe (the salutation is applied loosely too outside of marriage)
Sosoti – fleshy white fruit (berries) that grow on a multi-stemmed bush indigenous to Zimbabwe (scientific names: Flueggea microcarpa / obovata / senensis; Phyllanthus virosus; Securinega virosa)
Svondo – Sunday; a week
Tanhatu – six
Tatu – three
Tototo – a drink made from a concoction of spirits with a very high alcohol content
Zhezha – Rainy season (season of the year)
Zvita – December

Shona names

Bhusvumani – a common name used by the Shona for male cattle
Chidhumbudede – a Shona name which means "skin hide apron that quivers"
Chifedza – Shona praise name for females of the fish totem
Chisanhu – a Shona name which means "little axe"
Chisiyawasiya – a Shona name which means "passing the baton"
Dziva – Shona praise name for males of the fish totem, which literally means "a pond/pool"
Gwethlava – a draft cattle name made up by the poet, which means "of the whip"
Jekanyika – a Shona name which means "nomad of the land"
Koni – short for Konistenzi, derived from the English female name "Constance"
Kuvhirimara – a Shona name meaning "insolent and arrogant"
Madhuve – Shona praise name for females of the zebra totem
Majange – a Shona name derived from the word "*majandu*" which means "babycorn"
Makwiramiti – Shona praise name for males of the monkey totem, which literally means "climber of trees"
Manyuchi – a befitting Shona praise name made-up by the poet for the singer Beyonce Knowles, illustrating that Beyoncé is Queen Bey (bee), a female icon who empowers other women. Manyuchi literally means "of many bees"
Masiziva – Shona praise name for females of the fish totem
Mazvimbakupa – Shona praise name for males of the zebra totem
Misiinosiyana – Shona name which means days are never the same
Mukanya – Shona praise name for males of the monkey totem
Musaigwa – Shona praise name for males of the fish totem, which literally means "do not fight it"
Musingawandi – a Shona name which means "you do not multiply"
Ngowa – a Shona name for the Ngowa tribe, which literally means "just fell"
Pfumojena – Shona praise name for males of the monkey totem
Ravhu – short for Ravhuness, derived from the English female name Loveness
Rumbidzai – a Shona name which means "praise"
Save – Shona praise name for males of the fish totem, derived from Save river
Shanyurai – a Shona name which means "to plough in previously broadcast seed"

Soko – Shona praise name for males of the monkey totem, which literally means "monkey"
Thulani – a Ndebele name which means "be quiet", be "comforted", or "be peaceful".
Tinofa – a Shona name which means "we die"
VaChifedza – Shona praise name for females of the fish totem
Vhudzijena – Shona praise name for males of the monkey totem, which literally means "white haired"
Zengeya – name of a Karanga king, which means "a fickle, mutable, giddy person"

Names of places

Bhuka – a township in Masvingo province of Zimbabwe
Chibi – Chibi is a colonial name for a semi-arid rural agricultural district in Masvingo province of Zimbabwe
Chipinge – a town in the Manicaland province of Zimbabwe
Chivi – a semi-arid rural agricultural district in Masvingo province of Zimbabwe. Chivi was renamed from Chibi after independence.
Gwitima – a business centre in the Chivi district, in the Masvingo province of Zimbabwe
Harare – the capital city, located in the north east, in the Mashonaland province of Zimbabwe
Kariba Dam – is the world's largest man-made lake and reservoir by volume and lies 1,300 kilometres upstream from the Indian Ocean, along the border between Zambia and Zimbabwe
Mapanzure – a business centre in Masvingo province of Zimbabwe
Matonjeni – Also known as "Njelele" (in Ndebele) is a rainmaking shrine (where Musikavanhu is believed by the Shona and Ndebele to reside) in the Matopos World Heritage Area, in the Matabeleland province of Zimbabwe
Mazvihwa – a rural district in south central, in the Midlands province of Zimbabwe
Mberengwa – a rural district in the Midlands province of Zimbabwe
Mukuvisi River – A river in the city of Harare which is heavily polluted and considered the epitome of filth by locals
Musikavanhu – an area in Chipinge; Also a name for God which literally means "creator of people"
Save River – also known as Sabi River, is a 400-mile river which flows through Zimbabwe and Mozambique. The river has its source in Zimbabwe, meets Runde at the Mozambique border, then crosses Mozambique to flow into the Indian ocean
Tokwe Mukosi Dam – a dam on the Tokwe River in the Masvingo Province of Zimbabwe
Tokwe River – also known as Tugwi River, it is a tributary of the Runde River, which is a tributary of Save River, in South-eastern Zimbabwe

Shona euphemisms, idioms and metaphors ("EIM")

EIM	Meaning	Poems
Kneeless ones /ones with no knees – *vasina mabvi*	White people were called "vasina mabvi" by the Shona because when colonialists first came to Zimbabwe, the locals had never seen people wearing trousers which covered the white people's knees	• Elderly white man – page 80 • You've gone Madhuve – page 111 • Child of my aunt – page 76 • Adversity – page 30 • Acting – page 114
Great agony aunt – *zitete ziguru*	The role of paternal aunts in Shona tradition was to solve social problems by playing the role of what we refer to as agony aunts today. VaChifedza is addressed as the great agony aunt as she would have executed the traditional role of problem solver in the family and wider community	• Your Highness VaChifedza – page 18
To pick the meat first – *Kutanga kunonga nyama*	In Shona culture, families used to eat communally from the same plate and certain protocols were followed during the meal. The eldest and "table head" would announce when it was time to eat the meat (which was a luxury to be savoured) and meat would be picked in order of seniority. It was common for siblings to negotiate the order of picking meat in exchange for favours.	• When will you return? – page 22
Child of my mother – *mwana wamai vangu*	Shona expression referring to a sibling	• When will you return? – page 22

Expression	Meaning	Reference
Eat a dog – *kudya imbwa*	A Shona expression which means to throw a fit, or temper tantrum, or an angry outburst	• The Puppy Ben – page 55
The only thing for free is sunlight – *chamahara mushana*	A statement meant to motivate people to work, because nothing in life comes without working for it	• Acquired through sweat – page 96 • Rat in the granary – page 62
Calls become inaudible /calls are now inaudible / deaf to calls – *hakudamwi anohwa*	Distracted to the point of shutting out the world / losing All senses, OR as long as you have ears, you will not be called	• Sleep paralysis – page 98 • Machonyonyo – page 101
Eaten/ate many Bs – *kudhla mabhii*	Read a lot of books or attain qualifications	• Acquired through sweat – page 96
Flies can't land on their lips – *miromo isingamhagwi nenhunzi*	A Shona euphemism for talking too much / blabbermouth	• Dolls and melons – page 92
Sharpen your ears – *kuteya zheve*	Pay attention	• Letter to the girl child – page 84 • Acquired through sweat – page 96 • Release the chains – page 47
Your words are in my ears – *zviri muzheve*, OR *mashoko enyu ari muzheve*	I hear you, OR I concur with your view	• Tripping - page 48 • Blessed to be with Vhudzijena - page 75
Thrives on thievery – *vanopona nekuba*	An expression used by the Shona when addressing (in praise poetry) men of the monkey totem	• Blessed to be Vhudzijena's - page 75
Whilst the donkeys are braying – *madhongi achikuma*	Whatever happens, life goes on, even during complex events	• Chop the onions – page 73
Drum piercers – *mabovorangoma*	A colloquial term for sociopaths	• Elderly white man – page 81 • Dolls and melons - page 92

One who only bathes on Saturday – *chigezanomugovera*	A colloquial term for prostitutes	• Elderly white man – page 81
Child / children of my aunt – *chana chavatete/ zvana zvavatete / svana svavatete*	Person from Masvingo province	• Child of my aunt – page 76 • Misfortune – page 28 • In the Lord's name - page 110
Musandizeza means don't hold back	A sexist term for a short or inviting dress worn by women	• Machonyonyo – page 101
Chikangamwahama is a chicken gizzard, considered a delicacy in Zimbabwe	There is a myth in Shona culture (usually imposed on children to tame their love for chicken gizzards), that consuming them makes you forget your relatives	• When will you return? – page 22
Feeling myself like honey (or sugar) – *kuzvihwa vuchi*	Feeling proud in an egotistical way	• Misfortune – page 28
Ask what your totem is – *kuvhunziwa mutupo*	A metaphor for challenging or painful experience or discomfort. Usually used in relation to bitter weather or immense hunger or poverty	• Misfortune – page 28
Spit out English – *kusvisvina chirumbi / chirungu*	A metaphor for speaking eloquently	• Misfortune – page 28
In Adam's style – *nedza Adhamu*	A Shona expression meaning "on foot" or "barefooted" (derived from the Bible where Adam would have walked barefooted in the Garden of Eden)	• Adversity - page 30
Numb Location – *nhamburokishoni*	A colloquial term used in Zimbabwe to describe anaesthetic ointments	• Adversity - page 30
Dig / dug a little hole – *kuchera chikomba*	A metaphor for discarding something wholeheartedly for good	• I have dug a little hole – page 112 • Ego – page 39
Pisses in water wells – *nhundiramutsime*	A person with extreme antisocial attitude and behaviour	• Springhare sort of sociopath – page 118

Vengeful spirit – *ngozi*	When a person dies angry or unhappy with someone, it is believed by the Shona, that they will return to haunt the culprit until their spirit is appeased through compensation	• Springhare sort of sociopath – page 118
Children have been playing with it – *dzakatamba nevana*	A Shona expression to describe the mind of a person who seems insane	• Acting - page 114
Possessed by a spirit of an ancestor – *kugagwa nomweya wavadzimu*	A common excuse used in the Shona culture, by (usually abusive) individuals who do not take responsibility for their actions	• Condolences from the bewitcher - page 103 • I don't know you - page 108
Miscellaneous behaviour – *misarinya / musarinya*	Shona expression used to describe mischievousness or philandering	• Acting – page 114 • My lord – page 26
She has become watery – *dzangova mvura dzoga dzoga*	A sexist derogatory term used when women are being discarded by narcissists, which means they have lost flavour	• You've gone Madhuve – page 111
Separate the grain from the chaff – *kupesva ndichifuridza hundi kuti ipere*	Editing and removing impurities	• Editor's note – page 12
Groan in situ – *gomera uripo*	When married Shona women suffer abuse or otherwise in marriage and complain to elders, aunts, religious advisers, etc (as is done traditionally), they are typically advised to suck it up and stay committed	• Man is a bedbug - page 64
Can't get out of dresses – *haabudi mumadhirezi*	A Shona euphemism for promiscuous men	• Man is a bedbug - page 64 • Child of my aunt - page 76
Divorce token payment – *gupuro*	A Shona tradition whereby a miniscule amount of money is given to a married woman by her husband to indicate his desire to divorce her	• Man is a bedbug - page 64

This collection is a feast for your eyes and your whole body – *uku kudhla kwameso nokwemuviri wako wose*	The poetry evokes emotion and all senses	• Editor's note – page 12
Gift you one on the nutcracker – *kupa chamatsenganzungu*	A fist blow aimed at one's jaw	• Boundary crossing - page 117 • The vandal - page 106
Be enough! Like bus fare should be – *kwana semari yebhazi*	"Kwana" has a double meaning - "enough" or "sane". In this context it is used as a pun to remind one to be sane, i.e. they should be as sane as adequate bus fare, or they will go nowhere	• Condolences from the bewitcher – page 103
Those long baths paid off – *kugeza kwabhadhara*	In Shona culture it is believed that attractive women spend longer than usual time bathing	• Blessed to be Vhudzijena's - page 75
Deflation by insects – *kudzikisigwa nezvimbuyu*	When insecure or bitter people bring others down in order to elevate themselves	• Beautiful just the way you are – page 82

Shona proverbs

Shona proverb (in English and Shona)	*Meaning	Poem
English – Travel opens eyes to new things **Shona** – *Chitsva chiri murushoka*	New experiences come from travelling and seeing how things are done elsewhere	• Misfortune – page 28
English – Never go to places where your mother is not **Shona** – *Kusina mai hakuindwi*	Misfortune usually befalls you in faraway unfamiliar places where there is no one to help you	• Misfortune – page 28
English – Made it through the needle eye **Shona** – *Kupona napaburi retsono*	A narrow escape	• Misfortune – page 28
English – That which is good must be taken as is, milk is taken without salt **Shona** – *Chakanaka chakanaka mukaka haurungwi munyu*	Beautiful things must be taken as they come	• Beautiful just the way you are – page 82
English – Beautiful calabashes sour the beer **Shona** – *Matende mashava anovazva doro*	Equivalent to "do not judge a book by its cover", or a fruit might look attractive externally while rotting inside	• Beautiful just the way you are – page 82
English – A fair woman is either a witch or a thief **Shona** – *Mukadzi mutsvuku akasaroya anoba*	No one is perfect, even one who appears physically flawless has some form of imperfection	• Beautiful just the way you are - page 82
English – A crow remains black regardless of how much it washes **Shona** – *Gunguvo nyangwe rikageza sei idema chete*	One should keep to their real status in society because superiors and subjects will always be of different statuses	• Beautiful just the way you are – page 82
English – It is impossible for a pregnancy to be aborted by coughing **Shona** – *Zvikoni zvikoni mimba haibvi negoshoro*	Do not pursue the impossible, otherwise you do more harm than good, and you may bitterly regret it	• Beautiful just the way you are – page 82

English – An elephant is not burdened by its own tusks **Shona** – *Zhou hairemegwi nenyanga dzayo*	Each person is responsible for the burden of their responsibilities	• Beautiful just the way you are – page 82
English – A kraal worm living in dung thinks it is a cow too **Shona** – *Zundu kugara mundove kwahi neni ndava mombevo*	One might strive to appear a certain way, but their true self remains unaltered	• Beautiful just the way you are – page 82
English – The place of birth is the place of life blessings. **Shona** – *Mudzimu weshiri uri mudendere.*	Being authentic will always keep you grounded	• Beautiful just the way you are – page 82
English – Every sin has a bitter end **Shona** – *Hapana chinozipa chisakazvimbira*	Overdoing anything will eventually cost the over doer	• Rat in the granary – page 62
English – Pursuing a squirrel's milk instead of cow's milk! **Shona** – *Kuchemera mukaka weshindi kusiya wen'ombe!*	Pursuing pointless ventures in place of beneficial more or accessible opportunities	• Dolls and melons – page 92
English – By its own choice, the tortoise has a shell; OR The burden of one's choice is never felt **Shona** – *Chidamoyo hamba yakada makwati*	What might seem like a burden to one might be beneficial to another OR, one man's meat is another man's poison	• Craving for mutakura – page 86
English – The old order changes yielding place to new **Shona** – *Kare haagari ari kare*	Old life conditions are replaced by new ones	• Willow tree – page 94
English – Things that do not end are an illusion **Shona** – *Chisingaperi chinoshura*	All things must come to an end	• Willow tree – page 94
English – Alcohol makes old wives wenches **Shona** – *Hwahwa hunopa hutondori*	Drunkenness eliminates self-awareness and leads to prostitution and other immoral activities. The dialect used for this proverb in the original Shona poem is Zezuru.	• Machonyonyo – page 101

English – A bone containing no marrow easily crushes **Shona** – *Chisina mwongo hachina ziya*	Light labour has light gains	•	Corona – page 49
English – They who diligently seek, find **Shona** – *Kutsvaka huwana*	Nothing sought, nothing had / only those who make an effort witness change	•	Corona – page 49
English – A holy habit cleanses not a foul soul **Shona** – *Chinohi regera ndechiri muruvoko*	It is easy to cast what is in the hand, but not what is contained in the heart	•	Corona – page 49
English – Bitter pills have blessed effects **Shona** – *Kuipa kwezvimwe kunaka kwezvimwe*	Every dark cloud has a silver lining	•	Release the chains – page 47
English – You may dismiss mbodza but is it not filling? **Shona** – *Muchasvora mbodza neinozvimbira*	Superficial judgement which leads to dismissing something potentially beneficial	•	Cakes with no icing – page 78
English – Every guineafowl wears attractive spotted feathers **Shona** – *Hakuna hanga isina mavara anoyevedza*	All women's bodily structures attract men the same / there is something attractive about each and every woman	•	Cakes with no icing – page 78
English – The child expert is the one who is childless **Shona** – *Mugoni wepqwere ndeasinayo*	Usually those with no children are critical of the parenting skills of those who do	•	You have heard – page 52
English – The goat herder is given the ears **Shona** – *Mufudzi wembudzi anopuwa zheve*	A thankless job / when a beast is killed in Shona culture, the herder must be gifted a cut of the animal, but they are usually given inferior cuts, like ears	•	You have heard – page 52
English – In the face of dire need, a lion preys on a tortoise **Shona** – *Shumba kushaiwa mhembgwe inodhla hamba*	Chaff makes a good substitute for corn / in times of need, one ought to improvise	•	Using each other – page 54

English – An impotent husband is constantly annoyed by the face of the wife he married **Shona** – *Ijinyu rengomwa inosembugwa nokutarira chiso chomukadzi wayakarovora*	An impotent or barren man is constantly rough tongued to his wife / usually a man at fault passes the blame to his wife	• Man is a bed bug – page 64
English – A wife bravely bears all nagging from her husband **Shona** – *Kurumwa netsikidzi rambira mumba*	Retreating from a fierce battle is not to conquer it / spouses are expected to face the challenge of marriage with courage	• Man is a bed bug – page 64
English – Domestic frictions strengthen domestic living **Shona** – *Kugwa ndiko kuvaka, murume nomukadzi vanogwa vachibikirana*	Disagreements should not lead to severing of relationships / people should agree to disagree	• Man is a bed bug – page 64
English – Being bitten by the thing she dug up herself **Shona** – *Kurumwa nechokuchera*	A self-inflicted wound	• Man is a bed bug – page 64
English – It is roofs that conceal domestic squabbles **Shona** – *Chakafukidza dzimba matenga*	Do not air your dirty laundry	• Possessed by the spirit of Manyuchi – page 70
English – When he who used to eat dry starch now eats it with meat **Shona** – *Chaitemura choseva*	When poverty turns to riches	• Child of my aunt – page 76
English – Trailing blindly where we are persecuted like mice **Shona** – *Vanongotevera kwavanorobgwa matumbu sembeva*	Emulating or worshipping things that are harmful or not beneficial	• Interview – page 131
English – A lizard suns itself within view of its hiding place **Shona** – *Chikorovonjo chakangwara hachitambiri kure nemwena wacho.*	Before a man exposes himself to danger he makes sure that an escape is possible	• Interview – page 132
English – Cease measuring the snake with bark fibre **Shona** – *Iwe chirega zvekuyera nyoka negavi*	Do not waste any more time	• Editor's note – page 12

English – Eye-witnessing produces a fuller account of an event than hearsay **Shona** – *ndodziya mbare dzokumusana dzakarebgwa navakuru vakainda.*	It is better to experience something for oneself so that you form your own opinion	• Interview – page 131
English – Cease measuring the snake with bark fibre **Shona** – *Iwe chirega zvekuyera nyoka negavi*	Do not waste any more time	• Editor's note – page 12

*****Several meanings were sourced (and paraphrased or enhanced) from SHONA PROVERBS – Palm Oil With Which African Words Are Eaten – NM Bhebe and A Viriri published 2012**

www.ingramcontent.com/pod-product-compliance
Lightning Source LLC
LaVergne TN
LVHW041638060526
838200LV00040B/1621